Working Smart

Problem-Solving Strategies for School Leaders

Sharon D. Kruse

D1606696

ROWMAN & LITTLEFIELD EDUCATION
Lanham • New York • Toronto • Plymouth, UK

Published in the United States of America
by Rowman & Littlefield Education
A Division of Rowman & Littlefield Publishers, Inc.
A wholly owned subsidiary of The Rowman & Littlefield Publishing Group, Inc.
4501 Forbes Boulevard, Suite 200, Lanham, Maryland 20706
www.rowmaneducation.com

Estover Road
Plymouth PL6 7PY
United Kingdom

British Library Cataloguing in Publication Information Available

Library of Congress Cataloging-in-Publication Data

Kruse, Sharon D.
  Working smart : problem-solving strategies for school leaders / Sharon D. Kruse.
    p. cm.
  Includes bibliographical references and index.
  ISBN 978-1-60709-244-5 (cloth : alk. paper) — ISBN 978-1-60709-245-2 (pbk. : alk.
paper) — ISBN 978-1-60709-246-9 (electronic)
  1. School management and organization. 2. Problem solving. I. Title.
  LB3011.K78 2009
  371.2'011—dc22   2009005043

♾ᵀᴹ The paper used in this publication meets the minimum requirements of American
National Standard for Information Sciences—Permanence of Paper for Printed Library
Materials, ANSI/NISO Z39.48-1992.
Manufactured in the United States of America.

Contents

Preface

Imagine a puzzle in a box wrapped in cellophane. The picture on the box beckons. The scene might be a landscape, a cartoon, or a complex geometric pattern. In any case, the unopened box promises that after investing some time, patience, and more than a bit of creative problem solving, the builder can have the joy of completing a challenge. Experienced puzzle builders approach their task in a focused and systematic manner. They open the box, dump the pieces out on the table, and set the top of the box close at hand. They sort the pieces by color, shape, and size and begin by assembling the outer frame. Pieces begin to fit tightly together as whole sections begin to come to life. With each successful match, they check back with the picture on the box, seeking out subtleties of shading, comparing hues of blue and green, and make calculated guesses as to how those all white pieces fit together to become clouds on the horizon.

In other words, they develop a problem-solving plan and follow it through step by step. Focused on the picture on the box, they place pieces together in logical and sequential ways, seeking the best fit and the most reasonable placement of the pieces. Quite reasonably, savvy puzzle builders don't hammer two shapes together that really don't fit nor do they try to include pieces from another puzzle. Patiently and precisely, they look for ways to fit the pieces together to ultimately resemble the picture.

Experienced builders address the complexity of puzzles by focusing on the goal and seeking the most efficient manner to assemble the pieces in the box. They *work smart*. Of course, this isn't the only way to go about this task. Thrill seekers might dump all the pieces out and toss the box top away — seeking the challenge of remembering the details of the picture. Still others might wish to make the task even more difficult. They might purchase two different puzzles, dump one on the table, and toss the box out with tomorrow's trash. Then they might attempt to build the first puzzle by using the picture on the second box. Success might not be guaranteed but they spend their days toiling away, trying to find a way to fit the random pieces together. While they might be working hard, their approach is not as smart as it might be.

Problem solving in schools functions much like puzzle building. As a professor in a school-leadership program I am often asked to provide technical assistance to schools looking to increase student performance. After decades of work in this field, as well as more formal research into school improvement, I have found that the puzzle metaphor helps to explain the variety of ways school leaders approach the task of school improvement. Successful school leaders, like savvy puzzle builders, take on the issues at hand and seek solutions that help them construct a coherent program, policy, and practice. They remain focused on their intended outcomes (e.g., their vision related to student achievement and success) and work to align their decisions accordingly. They spend their time efficiently, smartly expending their energy and available resources.

At the other end of the spectrum are school leaders that, quite literally, throw the box top away. Absent a focused direction, they randomly adopt programs and practices that appear to hold promise only to abandon them when early successes are not achieved. As hard as they work, they fail to make progress. Absent purposeful goals, the complexity of the process overwhelms and traps them in a downward spiral of poor performance and inadequate progress. Still others retain the metaphorical box top (i.e., they have a school vision), but they lack the necessary pieces to build a complete and complex picture. In short, school leaders across the nation fail to understand how to solve the problems they face.

Effective problem solving contributes to school leaders' ability to create lasting improvement in classroom and organizational practice. This book focuses on addressing this problem by offering a model of problem solving based on years of research and experience. The model:

- Focuses on identifying a compelling *purpose* for doing what is right and worthwhile in schools;
- Defines the primary *tasks* of problem solving; and
- Identifies three strategic areas in which leaders *work* to successfully address the tasks of problem-solving practice.

It is my experience and belief that school leaders are hard-working individuals who want to see their schools succeed. The difference between successful leaders, and those less so, is in *how* they approach the problems they face, on *what* problems they focus attention, and *why* they make those choices. In short, they work just as hard as their counterparts but get better results because of their smart choices and focused attentions.

This book helps leaders to understand problem solving in their schools. It offers practical direction and advice to school leaders concerning how to establish effective problem-solving practices. It places problem solving at the heart of leadership and the ability to respond effectively at the center of successful leadership practice. It offers school leaders not only the tools for building strong problem-solving skills but a reason for making solid choices.

Problem solving is a complex and dynamic process. It is linked to how you view your role as a leader and what you do as a leader. Because of the tight connection between problem solving and leadership, chapter 1 begins the book by identifying the direct linkages between problem solving and leadership. By arguing that effective problem solving results in increased student achievement and better school climates and cultures, chapter 1 develops the foundation for problem solving as the primary leadership function within schools. Chapter 2 introduces the problem-solving model and will develop practical understandings concerning the *importance of purpose* and purposeful action to organizational success.

Chapter 3 argues that the fundamental task of leadership is to solve problems. By focusing on a cycle of *identifying problems*, *initiating actions*, and *evaluating results*, the reader will learn about problem solving in school settings. Each piece of this cycle involves a *task* within the problem-solving process. Unlike models that suggest that problem solving is an infrequent and linear process, with clear beginnings and unambiguous resolutions, this approach to problem solving asserts that each problem-solving task is a part of the work of school leadership.

Chapter 4 moves the reader beyond the inner layers of the problem-solving model. The two inner layers address the tasks of problem solving. The outer layer addresses the *work* leaders do as part of the problem-solving cycle. As leaders identify problems, initiate actions, and evaluate results, they must engage in the work of *communicating with others, developing supportive structures and designing policies* that address the issues at hand. Chapter 4 focuses on the ways we talk to each other about problems and problem solving. *Effective communication* is a cornerstone of successful problem-solving practice.

Chapter 5 extends the theme of the work of problem solving. This chapter will develop strategies for leaders that strengthen the ways in which they work on problems related to the school as a whole. The reader will learn how to identify *systems* within the school that support a problem-solving focus. The ability of a leader to identify the problems a school faces and initiate actions to address them is foundational to the success of the organization. The creation of strong systems within the school supports these efforts.

Chapter 6 addresses how policy informs and influences problem-solving efforts. Constructing high-quality policy is part of the work of school leaders. Policy sets the school on a *course of action*. When school leaders construct policy they create expectations for how students and teachers will act, how instruction and curriculum will be put into practice, and how the school will respond in times of crisis and stress. The work of creating policy is tightly linked to the work of developing systems. The implementation of school policy relies on the creation of strong systems to accomplish the work a policy requires. Without strong systems, school policy cannot be realized. Yet, without clear policy, systems are often unconnected and without purpose.

Before we begin, a final note. As much as we would all like to identify and solve the problems that confront us and live happily ever after, I take a realistic approach. First, I believe that schools will always be confronted by challenges. Second, I believe that problem solving is a way of life. Third, I believe that school leaders who build effective schools take advantage of the opportunities that confront them. And finally, I believe that effective problem solving provides leaders the ideas, skills, and focus to make their schools happier and healthier places. Happier because all members understand and support problem-solving efforts and healthier because goals can be reached and important outcomes can be attained.

Acknowledgments

I began my career as a teacher. After eleven years teaching both elementary and middle school students, I made the leap to academia. When I left teaching many of my colleagues reminded me that no matter how far away I went I should always remember what teaching students and working in a school was like. They were right to send me that message; however, it turns out that it was unnecessary. Every time I enter a school, whether it is for the purpose of collecting formal research or to chat with a leadership team about goal setting or reform practices, I am taken back to the time when I struggled with similar issues in very similar settings. I am reminded that the people who work in schools, by and large, are there because they want to do the job right. They care about kids and their communities and they want what is best for them. This book is a product of those memories and my experiences in schools across the nation. I thank all the teachers and school leaders with whom I have been able to visit and work. Without them my thinking and work would be far less rich.

At Rowman & Littlefield Publishers, Maera Winters and Elaine McGarraugh were exceptionally helpful. Additionally, I'd like to acknowledge my friends and colleagues—Dyanne Drake, Sue Johnson, Shelly Gaski, Susan Clark, Sandy Coyner, Sally Gibson, Karen Seashore, Jan Yoder, and Susan Youth. Their encouragement, laughter, and support have kept me sane and inspired me to live my life the best way I know how.

Chapter One

Problem Solving and Leadership

It's not that I'm so smart; it's just that I stay with problems longer.

—Albert Einstein

If Einstein is correct, persistence is essential to successful problem solving. Certainly we can agree that how long we work at a problem affects our ability to solve it. However, persistence is not the only factor that influences the success or failure of our problem-solving efforts. In this chapter we will explore the ways in which school leaders can create the conditions for more effective problem solving.

In this chapter you will learn why:

- Effective problem solving is at the core of great leadership.
- School improvement can be thought of as a problem-solving process.
- Hard work isn't enough and why working smart is important.
- Problem solving and decision making are equally important.

Leadership creates advantage. When leadership is present, we are able to take advantage of opportunities. Conversely, when leadership is absent we are unable to take advantage of the chances we have to grow and excel. However, leadership cannot be exercised anywhere or at any time. Leadership requires a context. It happens *someplace*. Second, leadership requires that we act in relation to others. We lead in relation to *someone*. Third, leadership requires an opportunity. We must have *something* to which we can respond. Absent place, people, and problems, leadership is only an ephemeral concept.

1

Problems provide us opportunities to lead. When we are faced with obsta-
cles that make it difficult for us to achieve our desired goals, a problem is
present. Problems can be thought of as *the difference between what is and
what we want.* When faced with failing oxygen tanks aboard Apollo 13, Jim
Lovell's famous statement was, "Houston, we have a problem." The identification of the issues that plagued the spacecraft followed. However, labeling
the issue as a problem was enough to capture the attention of ground control.
The response of the Apollo 13 crew and ground support team is legendary.
Dozens of people worked tirelessly to solve the variety of problems that faced
the crew before delivering them safely home.

Problems require us to act. They require us to respond, to figure out the
steps and actions we will take to address the differences been our current circumstances and circumstances we believe would be better.

Problems require us to figure out whose expertise we can tap. Whose skills
are required to assist and who can provide the right help. They require that we
take the long view; considering the place we work, the resources we have on
hand, and the effort required to meet the challenge that confronts us.

Most often, we do not actively seek out problems. Instead, problems seem
to find us. Whether it is the flat tire we find after a long day at work or the
pending budget deficit, like Lovell, we find ourselves confronted with situations that demand our attention. We rarely wake up thinking, "I'm going to
find three problems to work on today."

Yet, successful leaders do just that. They walk into their organization day
after day actively seeking problems—big and small—to which they direct
their time and attention. They actively search for problems, viewing problem
solving as a positive and constructive facet of leadership. Oriented toward
shifts in the environment, they use problem solving as a daily exercise of their
leadership. Consider the actions of Barb Agathe, a high school principal.

A veteran principal, Barb Agathe likes to say she "leads from the center by
being at the center." Barb starts and ends her day by walking the halls of her
1950s brick school building. Faculty and staff welcome her presence each
morning and she uses this time to pose her favorite question: "Is there anything I should know about?" As students enter the building she checks in with
them as well, asking about classes, birthdays, the neighborhood, and the
school teams. She shares, "Everyone just thinks I like getting in their business. . . . But I do this to find out what I'm facing. If something happened last
night it *will* affect how the kids pay attention today. There are so many distractions to learning. My job is to move as many as I can out of the way so
they can get down to doing it right. I try to find where the problems are and
do something about them."

Agathe focuses her early morning energy on locating problems as they arise and then setting out to address as many of them as she can. However, she doesn't do this alone nor does she let day-to-day distractions overwhelm her. She explains her approach, "So if it's a social thing, I pull in the counselors and get them to meet with the kids. If it's bad behavior I might meet with the kid quickly or ask one of my assistants to stop by and watch the class a bit—just so the kids know that we know what they're doing. If it's academic troubles we'll pull in the study hall tutors. They all know I'm coming every day and asking for their help. I can't do this alone."

Agathe's approach is to address as much as she can before the "day really gets rolling." She also uses these small interventions to keep track of where issues are arising and how the school is changing. She says, "I try to keep a log. That way I can add it all up and see where we need to think about changes. It's all linked to our learning plan. I just try *every day* to get as many issues handled so when we have a staff meeting we can really pay attention to what matters and not waste time."

As the example of Agathe's school demonstrates, successful problem solving starts with the view that problem solving is a way of life. Solving problems provides us opportunities to develop as leaders and engage others in working to make situations better. Problem solving includes attention to:

- *What* we choose to do with our time, resources, and intellect.
- *How* and *when* we respond to the events that challenge us.
- *Who* we involve in the process.

PROBLEM SOLVING AND SCHOOL IMPROVEMENT

Problems arise from a variety of sources. However, none are as persistent or as sticky as those related to school improvement. Across the nation, student performance has been scrutinized and found lacking. The result has been increasing pressure to improve. Furthermore, data strongly supports the contention that educational opportunities are unequal. While there are differences for the reasons why researchers think we are in this predicament, consensus suggests that students in schools today do not achieve or progress as they should. (If you are interested in more information on this topic see Goodlad 2004; Hale 2001; Fullan 2001; Schmoker 1999, 2006.) Concerns for achievement are best characterized as concerns that students do not learn as *much* as they should; whereas concerns about progress suggest that they do not learn as *well* as they might. Furthermore, research suggests that race, class, gender, and socioeconomic status all play a role in how much and how well a student learns (see for example, Brady 2003; Meier 1995; Riddell 2007).

What follows is a short school improvement primer. These comments are not meant to be exhaustive. Rather, the intent is to broadly outline the ways school improvement data and the responses to pressures for school improvement contribute to the problems school leaders face. These problems can be thought of as falling into three distinct, but related, camps:

- the dilemmas testing creates;
- inadequate problem identification; and
- ineffective program selection and implementation.

Testing Dilemmas

Measures of achievement (how much) and progress (how well) are most often determined by the administration of standardized tests. Standardized tests come in two forms. They can be norm-referenced or criterion-referenced. *Norm-referenced* standardized tests are designed to measure *achievement* and to establish how individuals perform in comparison to others who took the test. Scores are usually determined by comparing results to that of a normative sample or "norm" group. Students cannot fail a norm-referenced test, since each student receives a score that compares the individual student to others that have taken the test.

Results are reported not in terms of the number of correct answers but in terms of the average score (sometimes reported as a stanine). Scores that report a student's scores as a percentage—"Emily ranked at the 89th percentile"—are the result of a norm-referenced test. Popular commercially available, norm-referenced achievement tests include the:

- California Achievement Test (CAT),
- Comprehensive Test of Basic Skills (CTBS),
- Iowa Test of Basic Skills (ITBS), and
- Graduate Record Exam (GRE).

With the advent of No Child Left Behind, many states opted to design their own standards-based tests. Rather than rely on a nationally normed test that might or might not adequately reflect the standards for student learning adopted in a particular state, many states chose to design their own tests. These tests can be distinguished from nationally normed tests by the ways they measure achievement and progress. Instead of comparing student performance to an average of correct answers, state tests usually compare student performance to a set measure.

Known as *criterion-referenced tests*, these tests compare each person's performance to a predetermined standard or criterion. This allows a community to know how well students do in comparison to an accepted measure of performance. Criterion-referenced tests are designed to measure how well a student has learned a specific body of knowledge and skills. For standardized criterion-referenced tests such as state achievement, proficiency, or graduation tests, a committee of experts usually sets the passing or cut-off score. The cut-off score is set at a level that measures *how much* of a critical mass of knowledge a student has mastered. States that issue a report card of passing and failing schools detail the results of criterion-referenced testing. Examples of well-known criterion-reference tests include:

- most licensure exams including motor vehicle driving tests;
- Praxis I, II, and III; and
- exams for airline pilots, electrical engineers, and the like.

Criterion-referenced tests also allow for *progress* to be measured. Known as *Average Yearly Progress* or AYP, these measures allow us to learn about the gains students make as a result of instruction and other learning opportunities. Unlike norm-referenced tests that only measure where a student falls in relation to the population of students who took the test; criterion-referenced tests can produce progress measures for students. In this way, we can determine *how well* students are learning in comparison to a measure of yearly growth. Progress measures, sometimes referred to as Value-Added measures, can tell us if particular groups are making larger or smaller learning gains. For example, progress measures allow us to compare scores when students enter and exit a grade level, focusing on increased learning.

So what are the dilemmas of testing as they relate to problem solving? The bottom line is that attention to student achievement and progress has created an enduring problem for school leaders. The intent here is not to argue for the halcyon days of yore, where principals and teachers could do what they wished, when they wished. Instead, it is to illustrate that our ability to test and compare student achievement and progress both *creates and contributes* to our understanding of problems related to school improvement.

Testing *creates problems* when we find that students:

- are not achieving as we believe they should,
- are not progressing as we believe they should,

- are not achieving in equal ways, and
- are not progressing in equal ways.

Testing *contributes to our understanding of the problems* we face when we learn:

- which groups of students are or are not achieving as we believe they should;
- which groups of students are or are not progressing as we believe they should;
- what kinds of knowledge and skills students have mastered well;
- what kinds of knowledge and skills students have not mastered; and
- the ways in which our programs and policies, curriculum and instruction serve or do not serve our students.

Inadequate Problem Identification

When confronted with compelling data, especially data that suggests that students are doing poorly, it is easy to declare that a learning crisis exists. However, when the discussion jumps to immediately offering solutions, important problem-solving steps are skipped. Simply put, *we pay little attention to the reasons* why schools might be failing. Instead we jump to implementing new programs and policies and fail to take into account the complexities of schooling. Furthermore, we neglect to consider the myriad of problems that may contribute to a school's poor (or good) performance.

In a famous *New Yorker* cartoon, two scientists stand in front of a chalkboard. The chalkboard is filled with an array of numbers, symbols, arrows, and equations. A small corner of the board is empty; it is clear from the caption one scientist is about to write a final answer in this empty corner. In the caption the scientist states, "and then a miracle occurs. . . ." Understanding the problems that contribute to poor school performance is a little like this cartoon. We are aware that a multitude of factors influence the academic outcomes of students. We just aren't very good at figuring out the chain of events that might begin to address the problems schools face. So instead, we adopt programs, implement professional development, or begin community partnerships and wait for a miracle to occur.

We often make wrongheaded choices from the start, because we *poorly define the problem* that we wish policy initiatives to address. Because problem identification is so intimately tied to how we see our reality, our choices are often influenced by what we *want* to be true rather than what might *be* true. For example, we'd rather have the issue be our reading series than one of instructional skill. Adopting a new reading series is far easier than trying to change the ways in which a building of teachers approach instruction. Similarly, we'd rather have the issue be the schedule than our course offerings. Although changing the schedule is time consuming and difficult, it is less challenging than revamping the entire curriculum.

Because it is human nature to want to immediately address the problems we face and because we are often under pressure to produce results quickly, we jump to the solution identification phase too soon. Very often a committee defines a problem within minutes and immediately shifts to deliberations concerning the steps to address it. Rarely do we evaluate our assumptions about the problem. By prematurely focusing on solutions, we can find ourselves solving the wrong problem.

Second, it is also tempting to define problems by implying the solution. We state problems as if the solutions are implicit. "There are too few books in the library for reluctant readers," inadvertently implies that the best solution is more books. Such a formulation inhibits thinking about other ways to engage reluctant readers. Reactive problem-solving efforts place us in the business of patching and fixing the status quo. If we are always patching and fixing, then new creative opportunities are missed.

An example can help. Several years ago, a middle school just outside of a large urban area was looking to find the cause of dropping test scores. Immediately, several teachers jumped to the conclusion that the problem was poor attendance. They pointed to the patterns within their own classes as proof that their definition of the problem was correct. A subcommittee was formed to look into potential ways to increase attendance. Additional dances, special field trips, and pizza parties were all discussed as ways to entice students to attend school.

Just before the plan was to be implemented a teacher decided to check to see if the kids with high absences were, in fact, scoring poorly. Data suggested they were not. More detailed analysis suggested that the absence rate was probably not the issue at all. Instead, the data suggested that many of the students who had not passed had missed the cut score by less than five points. A lunchtime tutoring program was put into place instead. Scores rose in the following testing cycle. Added benefits included an increase in schoolwide homework completion and an increase in the course grades students earned.

An attendance program might have benefited the school in other ways. As one teacher noted, "Kids can't learn if they're not here." However, based on the data, it is unlikely that an attendance program would have produced the intended results. Instead, the tutoring program addressed the problem most closely linked to the data that first caused concern.

Inadequate problem identification *causes* problems when:

• the wrong problem is identified,
• time and effort are wasted addressing the wrong issues, and
• expected results are not achieved.

Program Selection and Implementation

Attracted by the possibilities, the allure of adopting a new program often overshadows our understanding of the problems within the school. Once a school (or district) has made the decision to adopt a reform, it then must take up the challenges of implementation. In the ideal setting, we select an innovation that is well matched to the issues and problems at hand; offer appropriate professional development and implementation proceeds flawlessly. Student-learning gains follow in easily demonstrative and measurable ways.

Experience, however, suggests that reality is far from the ideal. Programs can be poorly chosen for the issues at hand. A phonics program cannot address issues of comprehension. Our expectations for the programs we choose may be unrealistic. Students cannot learn algebra if they have not mastered the prerequisite knowledge and skills. Moreover, schools and districts across the country have a long history of poor implementation of school improvement initiatives and programs. The process of how we bring new programs and policies into the existing culture of the school matters.

If we think of these as tandem concerns, several outcomes are possible. It is possible to do everything well and obtain good results. However, we can choose good programs but implement them poorly. We can spend a good deal of time implementing a program that is not well matched to our needs. The choices we make about programs and the ways we implement them can forestall or contribute to problems in our schools. As table 1.1 illustrates, our program and implementation choices can include:

• effective program/effective implementation,
• effective program/ineffective implementation,
• ineffective program/effective implementation, and
• ineffective program/ineffective implementation.

Issues Related to Program Adoption

In an ideal situation, programs are chosen that are good matches for the issues at hand. If reading is an issue, a high-quality, well-suited program is selected. If the concern is reaching struggling learners, professional develop-

Table 1.1. Implementation and Adoption Outcomes

		Program Adoption Outcomes	
		Effective Program Choice	*Ineffective Program Choice*
Potential Implementation Outcomes	Effective Implementation Activities and Processes	Problem-solving knowledge, skills, and abilities are strengthened as new knowledge and skill sets are incorporated into current practices. Trust is enhanced.	Problem-solving knowledge, skills, and abilities are fragmented when time and resources do not provide the expected results. Personal trust maybe retained but the belief that we can collectively do better is tested.
	Ineffective Implementation Activities and Processes	Problem-solving knowledge, skills, and abilities are disjointed when even effective results may not be considered not worth the costs of attainment. Trust may be lost and learning uneven and irregular.	Problem-solving knowledge, skills, and abilities are eroded when focus is lost, trust is misspent, and resources are wasted.

ment is offered that engages faculty and staff in meeting student needs. If the problem is defined as needing common assessments to understand the ways in which district programs affect student learning across classrooms and buildings, then carefully crafted assessments are designed and developed.

Making effective program choices is not difficult. Carefully looking at the data, defining the problem correctly, and choosing a program that addresses the problem are all activities that help leaders in choosing an effective program. Visiting schools with effective programs can offer much to help school leaders understand what it takes to implement a program effectively and keep it running. Surveying staff, faculty, parents, and community members about the kinds of learning opportunities they would like to see in schools can provide useful data. Piloting programs and evaluating the outcomes can also help. Combining two or three of these approaches increases the likelihood that an effective program choice will result.

When effective programs are adopted, people who work and learn in schools benefit. Students learn more. Trust is enhanced. Efficacy is developed. School leaders, teachers, staff, and parents learn from their problem-solving efforts. They develop patterns of behavior and knowledge-generation skills that transfer to other problem-solving situations.

Unfortunately, making ineffective program choices is easy as well. No one sets out to make a bad program choice. New programs (even ineffective ones) cost a school or district resources. No one likes to waste time or money. Neither do we wish to squander the trust and respect of our community. However, ineffective programs get adopted for a variety of common reasons. These reasons include:

- *Embracing quick fixes:* The old adage, "If it seems too good to be true it probably is," persists for good reason. Lasting change takes time and sustained effort. Embracing a quick fix fosters a belief in leaders that problems can be solved without a good deal of effort. Instead, quick fixes often weaken the school's ability to engage in real problem solving by nurturing false hope.
- *Following the crowd:* Fads in curriculum and instruction change as quickly as fads do on the fashion runway. Generally, the popularity of innovations rises and falls in relation to the amount of press a problem receives. When school violence is on the front pages, bullying, safety, and violence prevention programs proliferate. When the media suggests that jobs in science, technology, engineering, and mathematics (STEM) are being exported overseas, programs to foster increased interest in technology, math, or science abound. This is not to say that school safety and violence prevention or STEM programs are bad or that they might not meet the current needs of some schools. However, more often that not programs are adopted because we fall victim to believing that others can define our problems better than we can ourselves. When we follow the crowd, we are less likely to be effective because our attentions are focused in the wrong places.
- *The shiny object effect:* Similar to following the crowd, the shiny object effect suggests that we must attend to every innovation that comes along. When we are attracted to every brochure, event, and idea that passes across our desks it is impossible to retain a focus on that which matters. By allowing our attentions to be pulled in dozens of directions we lose track of the commonly held values that make our school unique. We over adopt. In turn, our problem-solving effectiveness dwindles as we lose concentration on core goals.
- *Taking the easy way out:* Real change takes time, energy, and hard work. It takes learning about "Who we are and where we want to go." It is tempting to adopt the superficial aspects of an innovation. Incorporating the buzzwords that accompany professional-development activities but not the actions or intent that underlie new practices does little to enhance student-learning outcomes. When we adopt slogans about practice rather than real changes in practice, little changes. *People's problem-solving skills increase*

when they engage in sustained learning that challenges their assumptions and provides better avenues to achieve results.

Issues Related to Program Implementation

The key to adopting effective programs and practices is to choose offerings that are well aligned with our problems. In this way, the potential for our choices to meet our needs is enhanced. However, if we do not implement the program well, it may have little effect. Well-implemented, good programs stand the best chance of success. When we pay attention to how a program will be rolled out, how faculty and staff will learn to best use the materials and ideas included, and the ways in which we will monitor results, program adoptions have the most potential for success.

When programs are well implemented several things occur:

- A need has been established and faculty and staff, parent and community members are on board with the proposed changes.
- Programs are chosen that align with the needs of teachers and students within the district and building.
- Appropriate in-service training, held over the course of several months, has been planned and is delivered.
- Materials have been purchased and are available for use.
- Finally, a program for assessment and progress monitoring has been developed and put into place.

When programs and practices are implemented well, trust is enhanced. Learning is improved. Personal and organizational efficacy is heightened. In short, by doing the process well, organizational outcomes are better. Members of the school community learn, not only how to problem solve, but also how to work together to create shared success.

Unfortunately, ineffective program implementation happens all too often in schools. We spend all our time, resources, and energy in the adoption process and forget that deciding is only half of the equation. It is as if we buy a car, drive it home, but never put gas in it. Our choice of vehicle has the potential to take us to great and exciting places but it remains stuck in the garage because we failed to realize that it required fuel. Effective program implementation requires fuel as well. However, this point gets forgotten due to the following errors of organizational focus:

- Attending to the resource rather than to the issue it is meant to resolve: When we fail to define the problem correctly we attach ourselves to the thing we expect will rescue us from our issue of concern. Just as people become convinced that new toys will make them happy, educators become convinced that new practices and products will in and of themselves enhance student achievement. As we have learned in our lives beyond the schoolhouse, new things rarely provide us the happiness we seek unless we make other changes in our lives. The same is true for educational programs and practices. If we adopt a new physics text but fail to change the amount of lab work in which students engage, they will not understand or apply the scientific method any better. If we adopt a new math series but continue to stress computation over higher-order concepts, our students will not improve their complex mathematical problem solving. We may need new and better curriculum materials. However, effectiveness requires attention to both what we adopt and how we choose to use the adoption to meet our expressed goals.

- Forgetting the people that must work with new ideas and products: In our excitement to adopt the next new program or policy we often forget that people—teachers, faculty, and staff, parents and students—must use the materials and ideas we have chosen. When we make shifts in "how we do things" and fail to adequately instruct others about the changes these new programs require we compromise trust within our schools. Leaders risk being seen as uncaring: "Look at all the work that has been foisted on us"; incompetent: "They should have known then it wasn't going to work"; and dishonest: "They lied when they said this would not require extra effort." Trust is eroded when caring, competence, and honesty are questioned.

- Not accounting for prior experiences and practices: Memory remains a core component of "how we do things around here." Whether or not we like it, we remember how well or poorly prior events have gone. We remember the last time an adoption occurred and how we were treated. New materials may have been introduced and then forgotten. Our hard invested efforts may have gone unrecognized and unrewarded. On the other hand, we may have been treated to an engaging in-service, supplied ample and timely support, and sought out for our input concerning next steps for program improvement. These memories can detract from or enhance our ability to implement new programs and practices. Our collective memory is important in that it allows us to draw upon events from the past to influence present problem-solving structures. When prior experiences have gone well we can subsequently remember what was learned and apply it in the current situation to good effect. When it has gone poorly we must purposely transcend past poor performance or risk less than full participation and support.

Program selection and implementation *causes* problems when:

- it is done poorly,
- programs are adopted for the wrong reasons, and
- implementation efforts undermine efforts to create positive school climate and culture.

Effective problem solving can mitigate these issues. By attending to solving the right problem, at the right time and in the right ways, effective problem solving can:

- enhance student-learning results and
- strengthen school climate and culture, thus making the school a better place for working and learning.

WORKING SMARTER NOT HARDER

District leaders and building principals have stressful and busy lives. Torn in multiple directions, lists of must-do tasks seem never ending. Superintendents, curriculum directors, principals, and others in leadership roles work hard. The sad fact is that working hard is no longer enough to get the job done. What is required in today's schools is *smart work*. Smart work is strategic work. It is planned work. It is work with clear purpose and direction. Smart work allows school leaders to address an increasing problem-solving load with focus and intention.

This book began with the metaphor that effective problem solving is much like completing a puzzle. Successful puzzle building results from the alchemy of several related conditions: having the right pieces, knowing what the completed puzzle should look like, and having a building plan. Like puzzle building, effective problem solving requires that school leaders have:

- the right programs and practices in place,
- a vision for school success, and
- the leadership and management skills to guide others to those goals.

Hard work does produce results. Working smart allows us to not only produce results but to do so in a coordinated and productive manner.

So how can we work smart? Smart work is the result of conscious, thoughtful, and responsive problem solving. Smart work is:

- *Conscious* because the work is completed with a critical awareness to the significance of each task in relation to organizational goals. Smart leaders attend to tasks in relation to their priority and allot their time accordingly.
- *Thoughtful* because leaders attend to the probability an event is likely to happen and the consequences of it happening. Smart leaders think about what they spend their time doing and the importance of their actions.
- *Responsive* because leaders employ reflective thinking in their problem-solving activities. Smart leaders trim their to-do lists, eliminating nonessential activities, and simplifying any that are unnecessarily complicated, lightening their load for real emergencies and daily attention to important matters.

Working smart allows us to *set priorities* and to *understand the consequences* of our choices. It is necessary to understand how important a project is to your school. The knee-jerk response to problem solving is to suggest that everything is equally important at all times. As one principal of a small rural school recently said, "I need to do everything I do. I just need to make it happen somehow."

As much as the principal believed her statement was true, such thinking does not help. If everything is equally important it is difficult to figure out how you should spend your time to produce the most beneficial results. The reality is that some things *are* more essential than others. This becomes apparent during the end of the year, when lower priority ideas and events are jettisoned to ensure schedules are met and activities are completed. The problem is that once you engage in trade-offs, time rather than *purpose* becomes the motivator. However, it is hard to know if what you are trading off might be of great value or not.

Setting priorities early in the problem-solving process helps you make those trade-off decisions along the way, rather than in an emergency mode at the end. Getting a program or policy half developed before you determine that it is a low priority is wasteful and frustrating. In one urban high school, the principal became impatient when the superintendent insisted on prioritizing building-level projects and actions. The principals pointed out that they often did several things at once, deferring some choices rather than risk dropping the ball on other more pressing situations. However, the superintendent reasoned that if they deferred too many decisions, the resulting practices and policies wouldn't achieve the results they were designed to produce. The superintendent's point was that, by evaluating priorities, the connections and interrelationships among different projects becomes evident. Once the connections and interrelationships surface, work can then be more coordinated. In turn, coordination leads to better outcomes and results.

So how can work be prioritized? How can the consequences of your actions be analyzed? How can we attend to developing conscious, thoughtful, and responsive problem-solving skills? How can we work smart? We can achieve these goals, as well as find time to get everything done, if we attend to each problem by considering its worth. Worth can be measured in several ways. These include:

- *Importance:* By considering the importance of a problem we can determine how much time and attention it deserves. Gauging importance can be difficult, as leaders must consider importance relative to a variety of measures. Things that are important to faculty and staff may be less important to parents and the community. Things that parents care deeply about may not engage the interests of faculty and staff. Students have their own concerns. However, there are some clear ways to measure importance. Problems that directly impact the learning of students are of high importance. Problems that concern the safety of students are of high importance. Problems that threaten the school's ability to make progress toward its goals and vision are important. By identifying what a school values and using those values as a yardstick we can determine the importance of any problem. By addressing those problems with the most direct influence on shared goals and values, problem-solving priorities can be set.
- *Contribution:* Another way to consider the relative worth of a problem is to consider the contribution solving it makes to the school. Solving some problems contributes more to the attainment of a school's goals and visions than do others. Figuring out a schedule that allows for additional tutoring within the school day for struggling students contributes a lot to a school's improvement goals. Developing a system that calms the passing-time ruckus goes far to creating a calm learning atmosphere. When we choose to address problems that make a large contribution to the overall smooth functioning of the school our time is well spent.
- *Understanding:* Some problems are easily understood, others less so. It makes sense to address the ones we readily understand and move on to those that are less clear. Although it is important not to jump too quickly into claiming we understand problems, problems can usually be sorted into those for which we have studied the relevant data and comprehend, those that require a bit more digging but can be mastered, and those that require quite a bit more time and attention. This is not to say that easily understood problems should be addressed and hard to understand problems should be avoided. Rather, evaluating our ability to understand the forces at work in any problem allows us to determine the amount of time and effort solving the problem will require. We can then work smart by creating the conditions that allow us to tackle the difficult to understand issues that plague us.

- *Ease:* Finally, some problems are easily addressed. A single phone call to a parent might handle a student behavior issue. We can draw on past experiences of working with parents and apply those skills to solving this similar situation. Others are less simple. Difficult problems require that we allot more time and energy to the problem-solving process. We may need to learn new things as part of the problem-solving process. We may need to engage in data collection and analysis to discover the underlying causes of a particularly trying dilemma. In any case, working smart requires that we prioritize our work so that we address those things that are easily completed and create time for those requiring more effort.

Before we move on, it is important to note that the conditions for working smart in schools are under the control of every school leader. Working smart requires that school leaders rethink their orientation to how they do their jobs. Unlike the images of leadership that paint principals as superheroes, able to simultaneously handle five phone calls, surf the Internet to find new instructional strategies, and monitor the cafeteria, working smart requires that school leaders *think and reflect* on what they do before they do it. It requires us to be less hyperactive about the ways in which we use our intellect and energy. It requires us to be clear about what we want for our schools and the students who learn in them as well as the directions we take to meet those goals. Working smart requires that we learn new things and that we employ those ideas in our practice in direct and meaningful ways.

PROBLEM SOLVING AND DECISION MAKING

In popular literature, the words "problem solving" and "decision making" are often used interchangeably. Problem solving unavoidably involves making decisions. When we select a course of action from a variety of alternatives we make decisions. When we place the decisions that we make within the larger context of the school organization, considering how our decisions affect what we value and our intended goals, we problem solve. Problem solving is the process of *taking corrective action in order to meet objectives*. More simply put, problem solving is the process of:

- understanding the contexts in which we work,
- setting goals for future performance,
- employing data to make meaning of the issues we face,
- making choices (decisions) about what we will do to remediate our concerns,
- evaluating progress toward our goals, and

- using our school systems and structures to enhance problem-solving outcomes.

In this way, decision making is part of the problem-solving process. However, the problem-solving process involves more than making a decision. It demands that we pay attention to the contexts of our work in schools and the ways our decisions are embedded in the day-to-day activities of leadership. Since decision making is part of the problem-solving process, both are important. Making good decisions helps us solve problems better.

In the coming chapters, we will examine what it takes to solve problems well. Placed squarely at the center of discussion will be concrete examples of how to identify and address the myriad of problems that confront school leaders. However, by placing problem solving within the larger context of the school, we must also take on the larger set of values that underscore educational leadership. Included in this list are values related to equality, human welfare, educational opportunity, and democracy. With these larger ideas in mind we turn to a deeper examination of the role of purpose in the problem-solving process.

KEY POINTS

- Effective problem solving provides the foundation for effective leadership.
- School improvement efforts both create and contribute to the practice of problem solving.
- Smart work is strategic work. It allows us to set priorities and understand the consequences of our decision choices.
- Determining the worth (measured by importance, contribution, understanding, and ease) of a task or project helps to contribute to working smart.
- Decision making is part of the problem-solving process.

CHAPTER REFLECTIONS

1. What actions do you take when confronted by a problem? How does your problem-solving orientation help or hinder your work?
2. How is problem solving approached in your school? Is it something that you are expected to do on your own? Who is involved? What roles do they play?
3. What is the process for program selection and implementation in your district? Does the process create or contribute to problems and problem solving?
4. In your building, how are problems identified? Are there structured processes for identification or is it fairly loose?

CHAPTER ACTIVITIES

This chapter offers three activities to help you begin thinking about problem solving in your school. Try each one and then reflect on what you discover.

Activity 1: Assess Your Problem-Solving Orientation

This quiz will help you focus on where you are and where you want to go.

	A lot like me	A bit like me	Not at all like me
I know what problems are important and which are not.	3	2	1
I have a staff that knows to bring me problems.	3	2	1
I have a problem-solving "to do" list.	3	2	1
I am always putting out fires.	3	2	1
When confronted with a problem, I know exactly what to do.	3	2	1
I like to think about my alternatives before addressing a problem.	3	2	1
After I work on a problem I consider it finished.	3	2	1
I have clear lines of communication with faculty, staff, students, parents, and the community to work on problem solving.	3	2	1
I have problem-solving practices in place, and the others I work with know what they are and how I use them.	3	2	1
There are systems in place that facilitate problem solving in my school.	3	2	1
I actively seek out problems while they are small to avoid bigger issues down the road.	3	2	1
When I work to solve a problem, I consider how new actions and choices might affect other things in the school.	3	2	1
When a problem presents itself, I try to see it from a variety of viewpoints including students, parents, faculty, staff, and the community.	3	2	1
I always follow-up to see if my solutions are working the way I planned them.	3	2	1
I view the problem-solving process as a challenge—it is one of the reasons I enjoy leadership roles.	3	2	1

Subtotal for each column

Column A + Column B + Column C =

- If your score is above 35, you are probably in good shape when it comes to your problem-solving practice. You can use the ideas in this book to help you hone your skills and mentor others.
- If your score is between 25 and 35, your problem-solving practices probably could be refined. You can use this book to polish your skills and learn to include others in your problem-solving practices.
- If your score is between 15 and 25, you are working hard but have untapped potential for problem solving. You can use this book as a way to realign your efforts.

Activity 2: Assess Your School Improvement Orientation

This quiz will help you focus on where you are and where you want to go.

	Always	Sometimes	Rarely
1. School improvement is a primary focus of my leadership efforts.	3	2	1
2. I use testing results to address issues of student achievement.	3	2	1
3. When problems present themselves I look for a variety of ways to explain why things might be happening the way they are.	3	2	1
4. I often adopt practices because I have heard they are effective elsewhere.	3	2	1
5. I use testing results to address issues of student progress.	3	2	1
6. When confronted with an issue I try to address it as quickly as possible.	3	2	1
7. When new programs or policies are adopted or developed I spend as much time in planning how they will be introduced and monitored as I do in the adoption/planning process.	3	2	1
8. I think my school is fine just how it is.	3	2	1
9. I use testing results to consider the overall progress of students in my school.	3	2	1
10. It is important for me to appear as if I am addressing the needs of my students as quickly as possible.	3	2	1
11. I have a set of procedures I follow every time something new is introduced in my school.	3	2	1
12. Others think my school is fine just how it is.	3	2	1
13. I look for differences in and among groups when reviewing testing results.	3	2	1
14. I like problems to go away.	3	2	1
15. When looking for a new program or designing a new policy, I find the program or policy that best suits my school.	3	2	1
16. Improvement is always a priority.	3	2	1

Results

Add the scores for items numbered 2, 5, 9, and 13. The total is _____.

These items measure your approach to using testing data. Chapter 4 addresses data in more detail and you will probably find those ideas in keeping with some ideas you already value. However, if you scored higher on these items than the other three sections, you might want to pay particular attention to the ways in which you frame problems in your school (addressed more fully in chapter 3) and how you initiate and monitor program adoption and implementation (also addressed in chapter 3).

Add the scores for items numbered 3, 6, 10, and 14. The total is _____.

These items measure your approach to problem identification and solution finding. Chapter 3 addresses these ideas in some detail and you will probably find that those ideas compliment your existing practice. However, if you scored higher on this section of the self-assessment, you may want to pay particular attention to the discussion of using data in problem solving (chapter 4) and to the discussion of initiating and monitoring program adoption and implementation in chapter 3.

Add the scores for items numbered 4, 7, 11, and 15. The total is _____.

These items measure your approach to program and policy selection and implementation. The book returns to these ideas in chapter 3 and you will probably find new ways to approach some ideas you are already comfortable using. If you scored highly in this section you may want to pay close attention to the ideas in chapter 4 regarding data use.

Add the scores for items numbered 1, 8, 12, and 16. The total is _____.

These items measure your approach to your school improvement work. If you scored highly on these the ideas concerning effective communication (chapter 4), supportive systems (chapter 5), and constructive policies (chapter 6) will be interesting to you.

Activity 3: Creating Space to Work Smart

Take some time to reflect on your current problem-solving projects. Over the course of the next few days list the ways you spend your work-related time. This, of course, includes the time you spend in school but it also includes the time you spend out of the formal workday. Write those items here (you may need to add more boxes):

Current Problem-Solving Projects			
Problems related to student management and behavior.	Problems related to instruction and curriculum.	Problems related to faculty and staffing issues.	Problems related to the community and public relations.

When you have completed your list, arrange the items you listed into the following categories:

- How *important* is this task?
- What will the task *contribute* to the school?
- How well do you *understand* the task?
- How *easily completed* is the task?

List the tasks down the left-hand side of the matrix on the next page.

Then rate each one on a scale of 1 to 5, with 5 being the high side of the scale (e.g., very important, easy to complete, highly contributing to goals and visions, clearly understood) and 1 being the low (e.g., not important, not closely aligned with goals and visions, hard to do, not easily understood). Total your score for each task in the far right-hand column.

Current Project Analysis Matrix					
Task	Importance	Contribution	Understanding	Ease	Total

Reflect on what you find.

- Where are your priorities?
- Where will you get the most effect for your investment?
- Where are you spending lots of time for little return?
- What tasks might be easily completed?
- What tasks contribute to the core goals and values of the school?
- How might you be working smarter?

Chapter Two

The Importance of Purpose

There is nothing so useless as doing efficiently that which should not be done at all.

—Peter F. Drucker

In this chapter we will explore how purpose can focus problem-solving efforts. When we lack a central purpose for our problem–solving efforts we run the risk of working hard without producing results. When our central purpose is clear our problem-solving efforts are more meaningful and directed.

In this chapter you will learn why:

- Purpose is central to effective problem-solving practices.
- Purpose helps to make your leadership actions meaningful.
- Purpose and vision are different.
- Purpose helps us pay attention to big and small problems by creating focus for our work.

Ask an educational leader to design a new schedule, manage a textbook adoption, attend district in-service, and organize a school-business partnership and then expect her to reflect on her practice? There isn't enough time in the day. However, reflection readies us for change. Without reflection, we cannot possibly understand *why* we do *what* we do. If we cannot meaningfully link our actions to a clear purpose for doing them, we lack any real motivation for completing the tasks in which we are involved.

It is impossible to coherently reflect on things that are unconnected. If our day is filled with tasks that we cannot quite link to one another, if each event we attend seems unrelated to other aspects of our work, if the work in which we are engaged is inconsistent with what we value, we cannot make sense of *the reason why* we are doing these things. Consequently, we respond by going through the motions, by attending meetings but not paying attention, by talking but not listening. Our work becomes unimaginative and rote. And we become stressed and isolated. What we lose as we run from thing to thing is the meaning behind what we are doing. When we understand the reasons for our actions they become meaningful. *Purpose helps us create meaning in our lives.*

Several years ago it became popular to encourage people to "think outside of the box." This idea was, of course, to foster creative responses to the problems schools and other organizations faced. Interestingly, as explained by John Adair, the phrase itself came from a problem-solving puzzle. The puzzle requires you to connect nine dots, using only four straight lines by never lifting the pencil from the paper. If you view the edges of the puzzle as confined by the nine dots, the puzzle cannot be solved. However, if you move outside the box itself, the puzzle is quite easy. Thinking outside of the box helps us to solve the puzzle. Try it yourself.[1]

Thinking inside the box is, of course, the opposite. Inside-the-box thinking suggests an acceptance of the status quo. However, the metaphor "thinking outside of the box" is misleading. Organizational problems are not this neat. They rarely have clean edges nor do they have easily understood directions. Furthermore, the metaphor suggests that only by looking outside of our current organization can we find solutions to our problems. It suggests that external solutions are better solutions. Most troubling, it suggests that we know and understand what is inside the box and have exhausted all the resources within it.

Yet, in most schools, we have barely begun to understand what goes on inside of our schools. We really know very little about how individual teachers

Figure 2.1.   The nine dot puzzle.

teach or the ways in which our students learn best. We know very little about what motivates change or how to foster collaboration within our own school. We lack the resources necessary to harness the imagination of our communities or how to maintain the morale of faculty and staff. Looking outside of ourselves before we understand what is happening inside is not only foolhardy, it consigns us to failure. Probably, at this moment you are thinking yes, but . . .

- Can't we find good ideas and import them?
- How can we be expected to design a unique response to every problem we face?
- Isn't it a waste of time to reinvent the wheel?
- Aren't there best practices I should be using?
- If our current ideas aren't working won't trying new things help?

The answer is yes—and no. Yes, because there are best practices that benefit student learning that should be employed. Yes, because other school leaders have developed good policies and programs that might benefit your school. Yes, because spending time reinventing that which already exists is wasteful.

Yet, the answer is also no. The answer is no because when we import programs and practices that are not well suited to our students and our culture, they rarely have the impact they might. When we make decisions without understanding the ways in which our choices align with our goals and vision we act at cross-purposes. When we create (or import) something new, simply because we wish to do things differently, we do not serve our larger organizational purpose. We cannot know what from the outside might help us unless we know who we are on the inside. Identifying our problem-solving purpose helps us learn who we are.

WHAT IS PURPOSE?

So what exactly is purpose? As the scholar Nikos Mourkogiannis writes, "Purpose is your moral DNA." *Purpose can be thought of as doing what is best and right.* Purpose is how individuals find meaning in the work they do. Organizational purpose helps us define our shared values. Purpose advances collegial collaboration and imagination and individual morale and achievement within the school. Developing purpose within school organizations offers leaders a compelling reason for making the choices they do and a vocabulary for talking about those choices. Purpose answers the question, "Should we do _____, because it will help us achieve what we value?" Purpose can transform an organization by providing leaders a problem-solving compass.

As illustrated in figure 2.2, the centrality of purpose to the problem-solving processes becomes evident when we think of it as providing a focal point for our work. As a central feature of the problem-solving process, purpose helps us work smart because it keeps us focused on what really matters. Absent purpose, we might engage in any number of activities designed to address the problems at hand but the reason for doing these activities remains unclear or is not compelling. As we lose clarity and motivation for doing the task, our focus wanes. We move on to other ideas and projects. Is it any wonder why many teachers adopt a wait and see attitude when new programs are

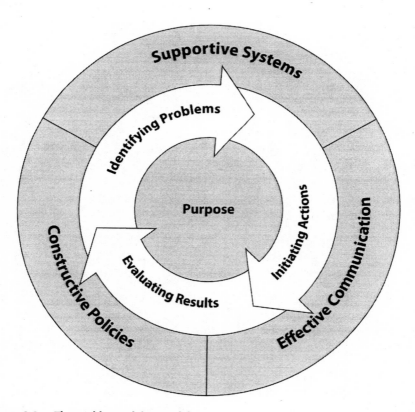

Figure 2.2.   The problem-solving model.

introduced? They intuitively know that when we adopt ideas that lack a purpose, those ideas are more likely to be abandoned.

Purpose matters. When we lack purpose we can lose our grounding. When we lose our purpose, we are a little less than the people we aspire to be. When we lack a unifying purpose, our efforts can become uncoordinated and ineffective. As hard as we try, we fail to achieve the goals we set for others and ourselves. When our purpose is clear and known to all, the potential to make progress toward our goals is enhanced.

Consider the issue of high-stakes testing. Scoring well is a goal that has captivated the attentions of educational professionals, teachers, and school leaders. However, attaining the goal of scoring well has played out in a variety of ways. Let's look at three—cheating, traditional staff development programs, and learning-focused (as opposed to testing-focused) efforts.

Cheating

We will start by looking at one famous study of cheating. As part of the initiative to increase student test scores, some states have adopted teacher incentive programs. These programs include monetary rewards provided to schools and individual teachers for increasing student test scores. Economists Brian Jacob and Steven Levitt assumed that as incentives for scoring well increase, unprincipled administrators and teachers might be more likely to engage in dishonest activities. In 2002, Jacob and Levitt set out to test how often cheating on the part of teachers and/or school leaders might occur.

Prior to their study, there had been reports that some cheating had occurred (Loughran and Comiskey 1999). Other studies had documented instances of allowing students extra time to complete tests, providing correct answers to students, or teaching students using knowledge of the precise exam questions (Jacob 2001). However, the Jacob and Levitt study looked specifically at tampering with student answer forms. They looked for evidence that teachers or administrators had purposefully changed student responses on answer sheets or filled in the blanks when a student failed to complete a section. Their methodology was complex and allowed for comparisons of Chicago classrooms across the city and across seven years of data (1993–2000). In all, they looked at more than 700,000 sets of test answers and nearly 100 million individual items.

Jacob and Levitt looked for anomalies in the data that might suggest cheating had taken place. Specifically, they searched for unusual patterns of answers for students within a classroom—blocks of correct answers that had been filled in following the identical pattern (for example, a, b, b, c, a). After careful analysis Jacob and Levitt were able to locate what looked suspiciously like changes on student answers forms. They uncovered student exams where students missed the early (easy) question items and then got a string of later (harder) items correct. They uncovered classrooms of students where every student had answered the same series of questions the same way. They ran sophisticated statistical-testing models to be certain that these patterns could not be the result of real student performance.

In the end, they determined that in about 5 percent of the sample, answers on student exam forms had been altered. In this small percentage of cases, the only conclusion that could be drawn was that the teachers (or the administrators in the building) had cheated. If we define *purpose* as our moral compass, clearly these professionals had lost their way. We can argue that the fault was not that of the teachers, that the pressures of testing had driven them to alter student responses, but that does not explain the 95 percent of teachers and school leaders who did not cheat.

On one hand, these results are startling; on the other hand, the fact that they found that 95 percent of the time no cheating had taken place is heartening. Said another way, almost always teachers and school administrators administer high stakes tests honestly. They find other ways to help students learn the material addressed in the test so that they might do well. But are those ways any more purposeful?

Traditional Staff Development Efforts

Another response to the pressures of accountability has been to provide teachers traditional staff development—lots of it. Based on a model of staff development that has been in place for decades, this approach employs a process where school leaders identify, adopt, and implement a variety of staff development programs. The planning model for this kind of school reform looks something like this:

- review the data;
- locate areas of need;
- adopt one or more new programs, practices, or policies that promise to meet the identified needs;
- lead in-service teachers for the new adoptions;
- expect the new adoptions to work;
- review the data;
- note that scores have not changed or locate new areas of need;
- adopt more programs, practices, or policies; and
- start the cycle again.

On the surface, this cycle looks _____
ploys best-practice models. It offers _____
dents new ways of learning. The only _____
schools, the process does not work.

The truth of the matter is that when people _____
often look hopefully to almost any idea that see _____
ing well, they make valiant efforts to identify the iss _____
them as aggressively as possible. They make changes, _____
variety of in-service choices, and hold parent workshop _____
However, these schools often fail to make progress. Why?

As Terry Orr and her colleagues have suggested, the factors th _____
to consistent low performance are not completely clear. Some sch _____
progress and then stall. Other schools make mixed progress, showing _____
among some portions of the student body and no gains with others. T _____
findings suggest that persistent low performance is marked by several factor _____
including:

- layers of partially implemented reforms,
- mixed capacity to foster teachers' learning of new ideas and pedagogies, and
- a pervasive lack of confidence in students' and teachers' capacities.

What happens in schools where persistent low performance is the norm is a slow and painful cycle of decline. Teachers fail to fully implement the adopted programs. Leaders abandon programs before they could be reasonably expected to produce results. Rather than engage teachers in learning about working with hard-to-teach, hard-to-learn concepts and ideas, structured programs that inhibit an individual teacher's ability to make informed choices about student learning get adopted. Individual building cultures and strengths get ignored as district leaders look for a one-size-fits-all solution. Finally, the volume of changes overwhelms teachers, students, and parents.

It is not that these traditional staff developers are trying to do things poorly. Faced with difficulties at every turn, they try to address everything at once. When everything is treated as if it is equally important, it is difficult to identify a compelling unifying purpose for the work. Without a purpose everyone can look to, it is difficult to stay with the work when difficulties arise. When teachers, leaders, and parents do not persist with reform efforts, little lasting change or improvement can occur.

So if traditional staff development models don't work, what does? How do school leaders develop purpose and address the pressure of accountability?

reasonable enough. It is data based. It em-
teachers new ways of teaching and stu-
problem is, for the vast majority of

are frustrated and worried, they
...s to have potential. Mean-
...es they face and address
offer teachers a wide
They work hard.

...at contribute
...ols make
...results
...eir

orts

is that *scoring*
en you decided
number of rea-

) share those in-

1 know and care

ate curiosity.

A basic problem
reform efforts is
that it does not align well with our purposes for waking up and going to work each day.

We all know that scoring well on standardized exams is supposed to measure how well students have achieved the goals of schooling. In this way, it is a proxy for the outcomes expected of the educational system. Those outcomes certainly include student mastery of challenging content and higher-order thinking skills. However, when "scoring high" rather than, for example, teaching children well or helping students to succeed, becomes the rallying cry, we lose interest. It is simply too easy to be cynical about efforts that seem so clearly politically motivated. It is too easy to ignore activities that seem at odds with the motivations we bring to our professional choices.

However, just as it is impossible to ignore the speed limit or failing to paying our taxes without getting into real trouble, we cannot ignore testing. So how do school leaders who take testing outcomes seriously meld scoring well with purpose-oriented goals? They focus on student learning. They acknowledge that the accountability movement, and testing in particular, imposes external standards on teachers. They concede that tests are not very authentic forms of measuring student learning. Finally, they admit that standardized tests cannot measure all the subtleties that high quality classroom assessment is able to appraise. And then they go back to the issue of student learning. How do they achieve this feat? Let's look at the results of one long-term international study.

Ken Leithwood and his colleagues Karen Seashore Louis, Stephen Anderson, and Kyla Wahlstrom have spent the better part of the last decade looking at how leadership influences student learning. Funded by the Wallace Foundation, they have studied schools in The Netherlands, Canada, Hong Kong, and the United States. They suggest three practices that are basic to successful leadership. Their work supports the work of other researchers that suggests that successful school improvement must be based in high quality curriculum and instructional models. However, they conclude that without these three basic practices, schools will not improve. Successful learning-focused leadership practices include setting directions, developing people, and redesigning the organization.

- *Setting Directions:* Setting directions allows leaders to help teachers and staff develop shared understandings about the organization and its activities and goals that can support "a sense of purpose or vision concerning student learning." Having such goals helps people make sense of their work and enables them to find a sense of identity for themselves within their work context. Specific leadership practices such as identifying and articulating a vision and creating high performance expectations help leaders set directions for student learning.
- *Developing People:* Clear and compelling organizational directions contribute significantly to motivating the work of teachers and staff within the school. However, they are not the only conditions to do so. Direct and specific attention must be paid to developing the capacity of others in order to productively move in those directions. Such capacities and motivations are influenced by the direct experiences of teachers and others in leadership roles, as well as the culture of the school. Specific leadership practices such as offering intellectual stimulation, providing individualized support, and providing appropriate models of best practice and beliefs are considered fundamental to helping develop people in school settings.
- *Redesigning the Organization:* The contribution of schools to student learning relies on the motivations and capacities of teachers and administrators. Successful educational leaders develop their schools by supporting and sustaining the performance of administrators, teachers, and students. Specific leadership practices include strengthening school cultures, modifying organizational structures, and building collaborative learning-focused processes. Such practices presuppose that the purpose behind changing school programs and policies is to facilitate the work of teachers and students and that reforms should align with the school's improvement agenda.

In other words, Leithwood and his colleagues suggest that having *a clear purpose significantly influences a school's ability to positively impact student learning.* Purpose is about establishing a direction for our day-to-day interactions and choices. In schools, that means aligning the work of teachers in the classroom with a compelling motivation to do that work well. Motivation depends on the ideas that drive us. By providing teachers and staff, students and their families, clear purposes for their actions, strategies can be framed that both inspire us and move us forward.

MEANING AND PURPOSE

Earlier in this chapter, purpose was defined as helping us to create *meaning* in our lives. We have examined how purpose can affect our practice by helping us to see the linkages between our motivations for doing the work and our day-to-day efforts. Before we consider purpose in more depth, we need to spend a moment thinking about meaning. Meaning is a difficult idea to define. To do so requires a simple example. What is more meaningful to us than our stuff?

As I write this, my basement holds about a dozen boxes of my adult son's stuff. Taylor cannot tell me what is in those boxes, but he cannot throw them away. For him, those boxes have great meaning. They contain the remnants of his past that he is not quite ready to part with. Taylor's boxes are important to him. They mean something to him. They have value. At this juncture in his life, parting with all that stuff has deeper consequences than hanging on to it. He intends, he tells me, to go through it all. When he promises to consider what he can throw away, he means it. He's just not quite ready to do it.

Taylor's boxes provide us examples to understand the variety of ways we communicate meaning. Meaning conveys *intention* as in, "I mean to mow the yard today." Meaning suggests *consequences* such as when we say, "This means trouble." Meaning confers *importance*, as in the statement, "That really means something," or *value*, for instance when someone says, "It means the world to me." Because meaning is developed in diverse ways, our leadership actions and behaviors convey different things to those around us. When our purposes are clear, the meaning of our actions is also clear.

When meaning is linked to purpose we are empowered to act. When our actions are purposeful:

- our intentions are clear,
- we understand (and are willing to live with) the consequences of our actions, and
- the importance of and the value we place on the work we do are evident.

When our actions are purposeful, it is harder to act dishonestly or unethically. It is easier to build trust and respect. Purpose allows us to make meaning in an otherwise stressful and pressured world. Purpose helps us make good choices because those choices are tied to things that matter to us.

A PURPOSE IS NOT A VISION

It is, however, important to note that purpose is not the same as vision. *Vision is about the future, purpose is about the here and now*. Vision is about who you want to be, purpose is about who you are. Vision statements clearly and concisely convey the direction of the organization. Vision statements provide direction concerning how people in the school are expected to behave and inspire faculty, staff, and students to do their best. Shared with parents and the community, the vision shapes our understandings of the things we offer our students. Visions also let parents and the community know the reasons they should value and trust the school. Consider the sample vision statement below:

> We offer the finest educational experience to our students, offering unsurpassed programs that prepare students intellectually, socially, creatively, physically, ethically, and emotionally, so that they are inspired to become lifelong learners and contributing citizens in our diverse community.

This vision is about what the school produces—inspired lifelong learners and contributing citizens—and about the ways in which the school creates inspired learners and contributing citizens—offering unsurpassed programs. It is typical of the many vision statements present in schools today. Inasmuch as it may inspire, it begs the question, "Why?" Why is it important for the school to create inspired lifelong learners and contributing citizens? Why should we value those outcomes above others? Why does our school do these things better than others? Why should the community trust us to educate their children?

Purpose answers the "why" question. *When a school has a clear purpose the vision flows naturally from that purpose*. Faculty and staff understand the ways in which their work contributes to shared goals and outcomes and the role they play in the school's success. Students and parents recognize that the work they complete is important and of benefit to their overall well-being and development. The vision is significant and compelling not because it sounds good but because it means something and we all understand, share, and agree with that meaning.

PURPOSE AND PROBLEM SOLVING

When we are clear about our purposes we are better prepared for problems as they arise. Furthermore, when we place purpose at the center of our problem-solving process we are better able to address our problems before they overwhelm us. What happens in most of our lives is that we address our immediate problems and we ignore the small nagging issues that eventually destroy us. As Charles L. Schultze, chairman of the Brookings Institution, suggests, we respond to the wolf at the door while ignoring the termites in the basement.

We all face lots of wolves at the door—issues that demand our time, energy, and effort. However, in all schools there are plenty of termites in the basement—small issues that the longer we ignore them become bigger and potentially prove more fatal. Table 2.1 offers several examples.

We can see why each of the wolves requires our time and attention. These are legitimately important issues and they cannot be ignored. We can also see why each of the termites gets left for another day. Smaller in scope, they seem less pressing than the coming ballot initiative, the leaking gym roof, or a classroom discipline problem.

The problem is that when we only fight the wolves, by the time we are ready for the termites we have lost the ability to tackle them. In other words, we've saved the schoolhouse roof only to have the foundation crumble beneath us. Here is an example of this phenomenon in action.

Geoff Weltter became principal of Edison Technology Magnet School in the fall of 2006. A universally respected veteran principal, Weltter was instrumental in the planning of the new magnet school. Working under Weltter's lead, teachers in the school were expected to use the technology-rich building to deliver a district-adopted online curriculum and to differentiate instruction within their classrooms. The philosophy behind Edison was to pro-

Table 2.1.   Examples of Wolves and Termites

Wolves at the Door	Termites in the Basement
Financial woes, levy failures, etc.	Declining trust in school leadership
Rapid enrollment shifts	A loss of morale within and good-will for
Decaying buildings and properties	the school
Building and opening new facilities	Scattered, poorly implemented programs
A changing and/or challenging student population	Unfocused, misunderstood policies
	A lack of community and shared purpose
Inadequate resources to address pressures for change	within the school

vide "individually focused attention to student learning through high-tech instruction." Hailed as a "school of the future, today" a full-page story ran on the front page of the local paper on Edison's opening day.

Almost from the start of the school, problems with the technology surfaced. Internet connections were weak or nonexistent in some parts of the building; district firewalls blocked access to Web sites students needed (although some students were quite adept at figuring ways around the firewalls, creating a completely different set of issues); and the servers seemed to crash daily. Although the handpicked teaching staff had spent a week at tech-camp to ready them for their new assignments, the recurrent problems tested even their strong skill sets. Furthermore, unreliable technologies lead to long periods of time where students were left idle waiting for an issue to be resolved and student discipline infractions rose. Frustrations ran high and teachers began to abandon the individualized high-tech instructional models and return to more traditional forms of group instruction.

Weltter found himself in the position of defending the school's philosophy and curriculum to the teachers. When teachers requested copies of texts and worksheets rather than the online materials that had been provided, he refused their requests, asking for more time to fix the equipment. Some teachers began to borrow materials from other buildings in the district and copy what they felt they needed in an effort to teach and maintain order. Others tried to stay the course but responded by sending unruly students to the office in droves. By January, teachers estimated that they were only using the high-tech curriculum 20–30 percent of the time and were supplementing with materials of their own creation or purchase. In June, over half of Edison's teachers requested transfers to other buildings in the district.

For Weltter, the wolves at the door were many—failing technology, students requiring disciplinary actions, teachers wanting to abandon the expensive curriculum model, and external pressures to make the model successful. However, when asked to provide a reason for requesting a transfer the teachers where unanimous in their responses. Weltter's lack of effectiveness as an instructional leader and his poor organizational management were their primary concerns. As one teacher commented, "Geoff is so wrapped up in making the tech work he won't do anything else. We're floundering."

As troublesome as the Weltter's wolves were, it was the termites that finally did him in. Weltter allowed himself to be seduced by the idea that once the technology was fixed, his other problems would right themselves. However, by the time the technology issues were resolved in year two, Weltter found himself with a staff that lost faith in his ability to lead and a school that was only marginally meeting instructional goals. He had fought off the wolves only to be undermined by the termites.

Purpose allows us to step back and view our problems as a whole rather than as parts and pieces. If Weltter had stepped back from his daily battles with technology, disruptive students, and unhappy teachers, he might have been able to remember the role in student learning technology was designed to play. He might have seen that supporting teachers by providing them additional off-line materials to tide them over until the technology was repaired would have assured the smooth functioning of the school. Additionally, he might have been able to develop the trust and respect of the faculty. In simultaneously responding to the wolves and paying attention to the termites, he could have won on both fronts.

So how can leaders use purpose to enhance their problem-solving efforts? When it comes to identifying and addressing problems, leaders can use purpose in three related (although not equal) ways:

- *Strategy 1: Wait for issues to arise and react to each as if it were a separate event with its own lifespan and cycle.* In this scenario, leaders focus on a series of individual responses rather than consider the ways in which they work (or don't work) as a whole. Leaders who employ this strategy may well claim to have a purpose for their actions, yet they fail to use it as a tool in their problem-solving tool kit. For example, student achievement may be our stated purpose but each challenge to student learning (the wolf) is seen as a unique and separate problem resulting in an array of solutions that may not fit together in any coherent fashion. Trust (a termite) is undermined when faculty and staff cannot find coherence in the choices made by leadership.

- *Strategy 2: Wait for issues to arise and then step back and see where they fit into the larger picture.* In this situation, responses are less disparate and discrete and more likely to, in the end, hang together. Leaders who employ "wait and match" problem solving are more aware of purpose as an important tool for solution finding, yet they weld it clumsily. For example, keeping student achievement at the fore, leaders may focus on those problems that fit neatly into a student-learning schema and ignore those that are less easily linked. In this way, reading might get a lot of attention while playground or hallway behavior is allowed to deteriorate.

- *Strategy 3: Anticipate problems and issues and take an active role in defining and shaping your response.* In this circumstance, leaders are proactive in thinking about how purpose can help them align the problems they face with potential solutions that enhance their progress toward goals. Leaders who anticipate problems step back from the issue at hand to look at the ways the issue is linked to others in the school. They then seek responses that address multiple issues at once, relying on synergy to heighten the effects of a single decision. For example, let's assume (in keeping with our two prior examples) that a leader's purpose is student learning, and hallway or bathroom behavior is a problem. Rather than jumping on the development of new policies written by adults for students, the solution might be to assign the problem to the student council as a problem of citizenship behaviors. It becomes the task of the students to then develop student-conduct policies and consequences for infractions as part of their study of democracy.

The example just provided is real. In Smokey Park Middle School, the principal, in keeping with the school's purpose, "Student learning every day, every way," asked the student council to develop hallway and bathroom behavior policies. Admittedly, neither was functioning all that poorly but loud hallways and sloppy bathrooms were of concern to the faculty and custodial staff. Tied to the learning district standards, the student council was designed to enrich the existing government curriculum. The council's tasks were to study the issues, design the policy, and inform and educate the student body about the new policy. The resulting policies (and humorous instructional DVDs) have proved successful. Teachers and administrators spent very little of their own time debating the policy and students feel a real sense of ownership in the success of the plan.

The development of the policy provided a learning opportunity for students while getting the concern handled with a minimum of adult attention or effort. It served the school's purpose. An added synergistic bonus was the involvement of students in the problem-solving process. By making them leaders in this effort, a policy was designed that was more palatable to middle school students, and they understood why reduced noise and mess in the school benefited everyone. In this case, the wolves may not have been all that loud. However, they were silenced and the termites were not able to gain any traction. Reflect on your school or district.

- What are the wolves at your door?
- What are your termites in the basement?
- How might you address the wolves so that they are held at bay?
- Which termites can you tackle?
- How can tackling the termites help you fight the wolves at the door?

INDIVIDUAL PURPOSE

When individuals are clear about what matters to them, their purposes are easily identified. As we saw in the list of reasons offered by teachers for choosing to enter the profession, the ability to make a personal contribution motivates many educators. Others are motivated by their curiosity for learning. Leaders also have similar purposes for entering administrative roles. Perhaps one (or more) of the following captures your motivation for becoming a school leader. Did you wish to:

- Guide others in important work?
- Make a contribution on a wider level or bigger playing field?
- Link schools and the people in them to the wider community?
- Be engaged with large-scale change and reform?
- Assist other adults in achieving their professional goals?

Once in a school leadership role, it is important to understand what you wish to accomplish while in the position. Having a purpose for your daily activities helps you to *focus* your energies and efforts, *persist* in your work, and maintain your *commitment* to that which matters. Some purposes that are the focus of effective school leaders include making their schools places where . . .

- students are cared for and about,
- learning matters,
- open communication about ideas is championed,
- independent thought and creativity are encouraged, and
- adults and children grow and develop.

We will now look more closely at each of these attributes—focus, persistence, and commitment—and understand how each helps us to lead more effectively and with more professionalism.

Focus

A key priority for leaders who wish to lead effectively is to maintain a focus on what matters. Successful politicians focus on the economy, health care, or international relations. Winning athletes and coaches focus on teamwork and strategy. Effective community advocates focus on safe neighborhoods. In each of these cases, success is usually the result of focus on a clear outcome or cause. Although the arena might be different, success in schools is not different. In schools where foci are more than slogans, faculty and staff, principals, parents, and community volunteers pay attention to the kinds of activities that directly contribute to attaining their goals. Their purpose becomes the focal point of their work and directs their problem-solving choices.

Persistence

Focus and persistence work in tandem. Effective leaders are persistent in their efforts. Simply put, they choose their focus and then they stick with it. Unless we keep our attention on what matters, we run the risk of finding ourselves off course. Once off course, our purposes are diminished and our ability to achieve our goals is weakened. However, persistence does not require that we do the same things over and over; persistence requires that we attend to the same goal in a determined fashion. In this way, we can shift the work we are doing without shifting our goals.

Commitment

Like focus and persistence, commitment requires a leader to embrace the direction in which they are headed. Commitment requires us to be excited about our plans. Commitment suggests an obligation to following through on what we promise to others. Commitment binds us to our purpose and to the choices we make about the activities in which we choose to engage. In this way, commitment is both an intellectual and ethical stance. Commitment is an intellectual stance because it requires us to adopt a set of ideas and work toward realizing the goals we hold concerning those ideas. Commitment is an ethical stance because it holds us accountable to the people we work with for our actions and choices. When we are intellectually and ethically committed to our choices we are less likely to discard them without serious consideration. Take a moment to reflect on your career choices by answering the following questions. What do the answers tell you about your purpose?

- Why did you choose education as a career?
- What guided you in your classroom to make the choices you did about instruction, the way you worked with students and your colleagues?
- Why did you choose to become a school leader?
- What guides you in the choices you make in this role?
- On what ideas or activities do you focus your at-work choices and time?
- In what ways are you persistent in those efforts?
- How does commitment play a role in other arenas of your life?
- How are those efforts like or unlike your work?
- Can you transfer what you know about personal focus, persistence, and commitment to your school or district workplace?

COMMUNAL PURPOSE

Communal purpose differs from individual purpose in that it creates the foundation for how members of the school community work together. When schools are able to align the purposes of individuals within with the organization's purpose, operations run more smoothly. For example, when teachers and staff embrace student success as their purpose, the school as a whole will be better able to take on a school improvement agenda that is aligned with student achievement and progress. Similarly, when caring for individual student needs is a core feature of an individual teacher's purpose, school programs designed to differentiate instruction are more likely to be accepted.

Communal purpose must be developed jointly. Once in place, communal purpose becomes a vibrant part of the school culture and climate and new members are socialized into the "way we do things around here." It is not necessary (nor is it wise) to reinvent your purpose each year; however, renewing your commitment to a shared purpose is probably a good idea. One effective way leaders do this is to tell stories about the school and its past successes.

Stories help to unite people. Think of the last time you told a story. It might have been yesterday when you arrived home from work or the past weekend when you got together with your neighbors. The story may have been detailed and long-winded or it may have been brief and to the point. You probably know stories you tell time and time again, at holidays, or when you get together with old friends. No matter the situation, we tell stories to convey an event or experience that was meaningful.

We also tell stories about our schools. When we tell stories about the school ten years ago, we are telling a story about our past. The story can serve to provide an example of how far we've come, "Remember when we only had one section of AP English?" Or it can tell us about an obstacle we've conquered, "Remember how we built the playground in one weekend? In the rain?" When we share stories about our past we can use those memories to bolster our resolve and recall the knowledge and skill set we employed *then* for use *now* to face our current troubles. Stories can serve to help preserve the culture of the school, but they also serve to build bridges between the past and future.

Just as our identity is formed and reinforced by the stories we choose to tell, our problem-solving choices are informed by our stories. If we see ourselves as the "scrappy school that could" we tell stories of how we overcame our problems. In turn, when troubles come knocking, we have a library of sustaining tales to fall back on concerning how we handled our prior difficulties. If we see ourselves as the school where "success is tradition," we can tell stories of how our past choices have provided us a legacy of which we can be proud. These stories remind us of the processes and actions we have employed and allow us to consider how we might use them again today.

Effective storytelling helps us to develop the underlying motivations and energies that influence the ways we work with each other in the problem-solving process. Stories can provide us models for working and learning together and reinforce three important aspects of communal work: professional community, organizational learning, and trust.

Professional Community

Professional community (PC) directs a spotlight on the relationships among adults within the school. As my colleague Karen Seashore Louis and I have argued in past work, by focusing on the goal of student learning, the PC framework suggests that strong school cultures are based on shared norms and values, reflective dialogue, public practice, and collaboration. The essence of professional community is that all adults in a school are presented with the opportunity to work with others to grow and change—and that meaningful and sustained connections are necessary for that to occur. This happens when teachers take collective responsibility and share a common purpose for improving student learning.

Organizational Learning

The concept of organizational learning (OL) suggests as teachers learn together, their collective engagement in the problem-solving process will generate new ideas. Classroom practices will be enhanced as a result. OL focuses on the ways in which new ideas are brought into the school organization, how they are considered and evaluated, and the ways in which school organizations retain and use the knowledge generated from them. Organizational learning generally occurs when groups acknowledge alternative ways of looking at issues. This occurs most often when the responsibility for problem finding and problem solving is collaborative.

OL, as a practice, is frequently coupled with the concept professional community resulting in the term "professional learning community"(PLC) (Hord and Sommers 2008; Stoll and Louis 2007). While structured PLCs have the potential to engage small teams of teachers in the problem-solving process they, like any other structure, are not sufficient to assure that *schoolwide communal learning* will result. Rather than focusing attention on developing structures where learning is to take place, a more productive stance is to place learning (for adults and children) at the core of the school's purpose. This enhances the possibility that discussions related to purpose will help shift the culture from old values and beliefs to new ideals and practices.

Trust

Trust is the bond that holds us together. Absent trust marriages crumble, business relationships fail, and friendships falter. In schools, trust contributes to our willingness to engage in new projects and practices and our willingness to honestly confront and openly discuss the issues that trouble us. Trust is considered to be the result of several dispositions working as one. Among these are integrity (or honesty and openness), concern (also called caring, benevolence, or personal regard for others), competence, and reliability (or consistency). Trust is low when leaders lack a critical mass of the attributes listed above or when we feel betrayed by those in which we have placed our confidence and faith. Trust is also low in schools that feel under attack by constant reminders that they are failing. In schools, trust among teachers and between teachers and other groups is linked to higher student achievement (Tschannen-Moran 2004).

When considered together, the themes of professional community, organizational learning, and trust help to build a strong foundation for school problem-solving practices. The outcome of engaging in strategies designed to foster professional community, organizational learning, and trust set the stage for achieving our shared purposes. Outlined below, these strategies, appropriately, spell READ.

Before we learn about the READ strategies, a note about them. The strategies are iterative rather than sequential and you may find yourself spending more time on one as opposed to another. Similarly, by including some of faculty and staff in each strategy you, as a leader, can draw upon the strengths of your faculty and staff without unnecessarily taxing the energies of your entire staff at once. Finally, at least as a mnemonic, "READ" links problem solving to learning. This is appropriate because it reminds us that the reason for engaging in the problem-solving process is to learn about ourselves and our students and to find ways to serve each better. In learning about our students and ourselves, we develop our purpose.

THE READ STRATEGIES

R = Reflect on Current Circumstances

When we reflect we see beyond the obvious. Day to day we make sense of the world around us by relying on our mental maps of how things are. We look for the things that confirm patterns we expect to see. It is only when something breaks the pattern that we stop and observe that it has changed.

Without the tool of reflection, changes can occur so slowly we may not notice them before it becomes too late.

Peter Senge popularized this notion as the boiled frog problem. He noted that if you toss a frog into boiling water it will jump out. Senge elaborated on this finding by claiming that if you put a frog into cool water and slowly warm it to boiling, the frog will not notice and slowly boil to death. (As an aside for those of you wondering about the cruelty of boiling a frog, *Fast Company*, a leading business journal, has debunked the mythology of the boiled frog. It appears frogs jump out once the water becomes uncomfortably hot. See www.fastcompany.com/magazine/01/frog.html.) In any case, the story persists because it is such a good metaphor for how we can be blindsided by subtle changes in our environments. When we do not stop to reflect on what is happening around us we are often caught unaware and unprepared for that which occurs. It is only when we look back on our incremental decisions and choices do we notice how they add up to our current dilemma.

On the other hand, if the scientists *Fast Company* consulted are to be believed, frogs aren't that dumb and in most cases neither are we. We don't have to slowly boil in our own errors and missteps. Reflection can help us examine our environment *as* we experience it. When we reflect on events as they transpire, several questions can help us to make sense of them:

- Do these events seem at all out of place with how we expect things to occur?
  - If yes, how so?
  - If not, are we concerned?
- Are these events part of a larger pattern?
  - Does this pattern look like others we've experienced?
  - Is the pattern expected or unexpected?
  - Do we think that the pattern is acceptable or should corrective action be taken immediately?
- Do I have all the tools I need to understand these events?
  - Will I need to learn new things to understand what is happening now?
  - If learning is required, where might that information be located?
  - Who might we need to contact to help us make sense of what we have observed?

When we observe what occurs around us we are better able to understand what is happening to us. Reflection can help us to understand how our responses contribute to (or undermine) our ability to attain our goals. This process of purposeful attention enables us to use the events that surround us as tools for building learning, community, and trust in our schools.

E = Encourage Participation and Discussion

Individual and group reflection is a useful tool. The insights we gain by thinking about what we observe can help us to identify and understand our problems more clearly. However, the process of discussion about what we see is equally important. When we talk about our observations and concerns, we can question our mental models. We can raise long-held assumptions up to the light and examine them for current utility.

Once we have begun a dialog about what we think is true about our school and the things that happen within it, we can begin to challenge existing ideas and begin to plan new futures. The process of discussion allows members of the school community to develop a shared vocabulary for thinking about the issues that are common across classrooms, as well as to learn from the thinking and work of others. Encouraging the participation of others broadens discussion and invites others into the problem-solving process.

If you are looking to begin a discussion in your school, don't start with a threatening issue (for example, falling test scores). Instead, start with a perennial problem all teachers share—late homework, blurting, tardiness, lack of engagement or motivation—by doing so you can develop much needed trust in the process. After all, if you want real work to be completed in a discussion session and authentic shared purposes to emerge, you will need to set the stage for trusting communal effort.

Ground rules may help the process in the beginning. You might consider suggesting the following:

- Listen actively—when others are talking, work to understand what they are saying.
- Stay on topic—when the group gets too far afield, agree to come back to the original purpose of the discussion, make note of the new topic for a future discussion time.
- Set a time limit—agree that the discussion will last no more than thirty minutes or so; if the timeframe is short it is more likely that people will leave wanting more discussion rather than feeling that their time has been wasted. It may also be necessary to set a time limit on individual speakers; you want to hear as many voices as possible.
- Actively facilitate—have a variety of questions and follow-ups to keep the conversation moving. Consider taking notes or assigning a note taker, refer to the points already mentioned, and ask for more details or information if the conversation lags.
- Take time at the end to summarize the key themes and ideas—return to the original question or issue at hand: "We were discussing tardiness." Then briefly note what was learned in the discussion: "We brainstormed poten-

tial reasons for tardiness and some ideas for how we might curtail it in the future. We need to consult with the counselors to see if they have additional resources."

- Promise a follow-up and then do what you promise—end the meeting by suggesting next steps. You can agree to try one of the ideas suggested, collect data that is needed to move further, or seek the help of others in making sense of what was uncovered. In any case, be sure to do what you promise and provide timely feedback to those that attended and participated.

By encouraging participation and discussion, leaders can broaden investment in the shared values and purposes of the school community. Today's schools require the work of a team to be successful. Communal participation in and discussion about what we value is synergistic, it reinforces our shared purpose and creates organizational learning and trust.

A = Analyze Available Data to Develop or Reinforce Your Organizational Purpose

Inasmuch as discussion and the reflection that prompts it are worthwhile organizational activities, unless ultimately we check to see if the data supports our thinking, all we have done is share our ignorance. We might feel all warm and fuzzy that we commonly share the same ideas; however, if those ideas are not based in the reality of our school, we delude ourselves and our purpose is not served. In this way, asking *why* things occur the way they do is a worthwhile activity for considering by the school. If you haven't already completed the why activity related to vision at the end of chapter 1, now might be a good time to do so.

Other forms of data collection and analysis will be discussed in chapters 3 and 4 so the point won't be belabored here; however, it cannot be stressed enough that good reliable data is a prerequisite for purposeful problem solving. As our ability to discuss matters matures, and as a leader you think faculty and staff are ready to take on more meaty and controversial matters, starting from data is always a good way to begin. You can present a small set of findings (start with something big enough so that it can engender discussion but not so big that it overwhelms) and use your already well-practiced discussion technique to pose the following questions:

- What does this data seem to say about our school? Our students? Our faculty and staff? Our community? Our programs?
- Is it consistent with other forms of data we have looked at (or know of)?
- What patterns can be observed in the data?

- What other forms of data might help us to understand the patterns we are observing?
- Is this data telling a story about curriculum? Instruction? Students?
- What other stories might this data share?
- If this were another school's data, what would you want them to know?

By focusing on the data and probing it for all it has to offer, we can keep the discussion purposeful. By *not* asking, "What do you think this means?" followed by the enviable, "And how can we fix it?" data can be used as a tool to develop other qualities of the school including community, learning, and trust. Purpose is developed and reinforced in the process as discussion focuses on what matters in the school rather than laying blame or deflecting responsibility.

D = Determine Purposeful Direction

You've reflected, you've discussed, and you've consulted the data; at some point in time you have to commit. Ultimately, as a school community, we need to take a stand and move forward. We need to state our purpose and embrace it as the compass we will employ to guide us through our problem-solving process. Remembering that purpose relates people—teachers, students, parents, and the community—to the plans and goals we have for the school, we need to publicly commit to what we believe is our reason for educating. A compelling purpose attracts followers and sets the direction for future actions. As you determine your purposeful direction, consider these questions:

- Can we state the purpose in clear understandable words?
- Is the purpose likely to engage others in our work?
- Does the purpose inspire us to work more collaboratively and reflectively?
- Does the purpose evoke something meaningful?
- Are you proud of the purpose?

However important a shared purpose might be in the problem-solving process it is only the beginning to solving the problems that face school leaders. Once we understand why we are making our problem-solving choices we must also act on our problems with care and skill. To do so requires that school leaders work smart. Doing so involves school leaders in identifying problems, initiating actions, and evaluating the results of their work in ways that promote success. Those ideas will be the focus of the next chapter.

KEY POINTS

- Purpose helps us create meaning in our lives.
- Purpose is crucial for coherent problem-solving efforts. When we link our actions to a larger purpose, our achievements have meaning.
- Purpose helps leaders create a vision that is meaningful and compelling.
- Purpose alone cannot produce results; purpose must be linked to thoughtful, reflective activity.
- Purpose allows us to simultaneously pay attention to the big problems (the wolf at the door) and the smaller but equally threatening problems (the termites in the basement).

CHAPTER REFLECTIONS

1. Do you have a clear purpose? If so what is it? If not, what might it be?
2. Where are examples in your life where purpose and meaning have been clear? What can you learn from those instances?
3. What purposes have been present in your school in the past?
4. How would teachers, parents, and community members define your purpose? In what ways are those definitions similar or dissimilar to your definition?
5. What are the implications of purpose for your current problem-solving efforts?
6. What changes to the ways you are currently working will be necessary to align your purpose and your actions?

CHAPTER ACTIVITIES

The activities for chapter 2 focus on helping you identify and develop your purpose. Although you might be tempted to do only one of them, they are most effective if you complete and reflect on all three.

Activity 1: What's Your Purpose?

Rank these words according to how well they capture what you are hoping to achieve personally and professionally. Rank those you value most highly a 1 and those you value least a 3. Completing this task will get you ready for thinking about the relation of purpose and meaning in our lives.

Attribute	Value as an/a...	1	2	3
Security	Individual			
	Professional			
Commitment	Individual			
	Professional			
Passion	Individual			
	Professional			
Courage	Individual			
	Professional			
Generosity	Individual			
	Professional			
Competence	Individual			
	Professional			
Curiosity	Individual			
	Professional			
Willpower	Individual			
	Professional			
Adventure	Individual			
	Professional			
Happiness	Individual			
	Professional			
Empathy	Individual			
	Professional			
Consistency	Individual			
	Professional			
Achievement	Individual			
	Professional			
Openness	Individual			
	Professional			
Responsiveness	Individual			
	Professional			

Now take two different colored pens or pencils (one of each will work), connect the scores for those items you value as an individual in one color and the ones you value as a professional inanother.

- What do you notice about how you ranked these words?
- Are your markings consistent?
- Where are the similarities?
- Where are the differences?
- If your colleagues were to complete this same matrix would they value the same things?
- What does this tell you about how you derive meaning from personal and professional situations?

Activity 2: Examine Your Vision

In the space below, write your school's (or district's) vision statement.
Our vision is:

_____
_____
_____
_____
_____

Now examine that vision by answering the following purpose-oriented questions:

- Why are these ideals important?
- Why should students do what we ask of them?
- Why should faculty and staff support this vision?
- Why should parents and the community support our efforts?
- Why do we offer the program we do?
- Why are discipline and classroom management handled the ways they are?
- Why are our choices about program and policy in line with our vision as we have written it?

Reflect on your answers.

- Does your vision rest on a clear purpose?
- Do all the members of your school know your purpose? The community the school serves?
- Does your vision need revision to better align with your purposes?

Topic: _____				
READ	*Who?*	*What Activities?*	*Why?*	*How?*
Reflect				
Encourage				
Analyze				
Direction				

Activity 3: Read Your School

Using the planning chart below think of an issue that can provide you a good starting point for developing communal purpose within your school. In each of the READ strategy boxes write down:

- who you might involve in each phase,
- in what activities you would have them participate,
- why this is important to the school (what the outcome might look like),
- how you will accomplish this task (what materials you might need, etc.).

At the conclusion of your work you might wish to bring together your faculty and staff to develop a purpose statement. Keep it short. Some ways to begin include:

- At our school, we value _____.
- At our school, our shared purpose is _____.
- At our school, we believe _____.
- At our school, _____ guides all of our choices and plans.
- At our school, our efforts are focused on _____.

NOTE

1. Numerous solutions to the nine dot puzzle are available online.

Chapter Three

The Problem-Solving Cycle

We are too busy mopping the floor to turn off the faucet.

—Unknown Author

As school leaders we find ourselves in the position of working hard at the symptoms of our problems without addressing their causes. When we fail to address the reasons why problems exist we are less effective as leaders than we would like to be. Effective problem solving requires that school leaders solve the right problems, in the right ways, and be able to evaluate the results of our actions. In this chapter we will explore how to identify problems, how to initiate actions to remedy them, and the ways in which we can evaluate the results of our efforts.

In this chapter you will learn why:

- The fundamental task of leadership is to solve problems.
- Identifying problems requires avoiding our preconceptions and predispositions as well as parsing bigger problems into smaller, more manageable units.
- Initiating actions includes more than deciding what we will do; initiating actions necessitates that we consider the variables of time, effort, outcomes, strategy, and personnel in planning.
- Evaluating results creates success.

The fundamental task of leadership is to solve problems. While this may seem like a somewhat brash statement, think for a minute about your work last week. Perhaps you met with parents to plan a new afterschool program. Maybe you attended a workshop on teacher teaming, co-teaching, or block scheduling. Possibly your week was filled with teaching observations and matters of instructional supervision. In all these cases, the activities in which you engaged were designed to address an existing problem or potential problem within your school or district. Afterschool programs help keep students out of trouble and enhance student learning. Workshops provide new information and skills that can help us see the tasks of teaching and learning differently. Observations of teaching allow us to reinforce high-quality pedagogies and to assist when teachers are struggling.

Even when we think we are engaged in matters external to the core purposes of our work, we are still problem solving in some larger sense. Attendance at community events helps to keep the profile of the school strong and boosts the community's awareness of the school. District meetings have the potential to bind us together across buildings and grade levels to commonly held goals and values. School plays, musical performances, and sporting events all help us to learn who our students are outside of the classroom and to create common experiences that enrich our in-school relationships with students.

When the variety of opportunities in which we engage are viewed as part of the problem-solving process, we not only reinforce the purpose of our work, but also we are provided an opportunity to think more broadly about that work. As we noted in chapter 1, when we look for problems and view them as opportunities to develop our schools, the likelihood that we will respond effectively is increased. Our proactive problem-solving behaviors prepare us for the day-to-day issues that arise. As Louis Pasteur is credited with saying, "Chance favors the prepared mind." As we prepare for what might come, we are better able to manage and lead every day.

Return to your mental list of last week's events. How many of them fall into one or more of these categories of school leadership behaviors?

- Communicating purpose, vision, and goals.
- Providing encouragement and recognition to students or faculty.
- Establishing rapport, trust, and respect with parents or the community.
- Obtaining resources including support for new initiatives and ideas.
- Adapting operating procedures or existing policies to better fit new or changing circumstances.
- Monitoring instructional, curricular, and/or assessment-improvement efforts.
- Managing disturbances or student behavior.

Your list might include a variety of other tasks as well. Some school leaders attend school board meetings, others teach classes, some coach, and still others serve as technology coordinators, curriculum directors, pupil personnel leaders, and special education directors. Whatever your particular role includes, at the very least, you probably monitor student behavior, attend a variety of meetings, set goals and evaluate progress toward them, speak for the school, and assure the smooth operation of the instructional program. When leadership behaviors are well executed, no matter the venue, they enhance the school's ability to function. Poor performance detracts from the overall operation of the school. Furthermore, poor performance can exacerbate existing and potential problems.

As table 3.1 demonstrates, every time you participate in a leadership activity you are given an opportunity to practice leadership behaviors. In turn, leadership behaviors are linked to the problem-solving process by providing a venue for the identification of existing or potential problems. For example, if, as you observe students in the halls, you notice an increase in dress code violations, you might decide to bring together a group of teachers and parents to discuss the policy. Or while talking with other school leaders you learn that

Table 3.1.   Leadership Behaviors as Evidenced in School Activities

Leadership Behaviors	*Leadership Activity*				
	Monitor	*Meeting Attendee*	*Evaluator*	*Spokes-person*	*Instructional leader*
Communicating purpose, vision, and goals					
Providing encouragement and recognition					
Establishing rapport, trust, and respect					
Obtaining resources					
Adapting procedures or policies					
Monitoring improvement efforts					
Managing student behavior					

teachers in their schools are having difficulties with implementing the new math series, you might chat briefly with teachers in your school to see if they are experiencing similar issues. In each case, early activity increases your potential to address the issue before it becomes unwieldy. When problems are identified early they are easier to solve and their consequences less dire.

Similarly, if you become aware that your daily activities are less balanced than the above example, you may be missing opportunities to locate and address problems. As we can see, there are many opportunities to establish rapport, trust, and respect, whereas we are provided fewer chances to obtain resources. This suggests that when we are given an opening to do so we should be sure to make the most of the occasion. Similarly, since most leaders spend a lot of time in meetings it is important that we are clear about our purpose for attending and utilize the opportunity to exercise appropriate leadership behaviors. This way the time invested can be best used to secure the outcomes we seek.

EXPLORING THE PROBLEM-SOLVING CYCLE

As you have probably already noted when we think of problem solving in this way, it is not an infrequent or linear process. Rather, it is an ever-present cycle that informs our daily work. There is good news and bad news in this idea. The good news is that by consciously engaging in daily problem solving, school improvement efforts can become a central part of your daily work instead of an additional or supplemental activity. The bad news is that you will rarely find yourself addressing issues with clear beginnings and unambiguous resolutions.

When thought of in this manner, it is easy to see how problem solving can frame the work of principals and superintendents in focused and purposeful ways. When viewed as a *contribution* to school improvement and student success, problem solving becomes a positive and unifying feature of a leader's work. When principals and other school leaders engage in leadership activities that enhance a school's ability to problem solve they are also enhancing the school's ability to be successful.

IDENTIFYING PROBLEMS—PRECONCEPTIONS AND PREDISPOSITIONS

Schools are complex places. Although each is unique, get two or more school leaders in a room together, and similar concerns will surface. Student achievement and motivation will usually be mentioned, as will funding and working with the community. Whether the issues are perceived as phenomena with serious negative systemic impact (loss of funding), or significant discrepancies in the system (unequal access to enrichment or intervention services), or as grievances related to the conditions of schooling today (achievement- and progress-measure pressures, lack of parent or community support), there is general agreement that common problems exist. Moreover, it would not take much to get school leaders to admit that these are big problems and even the best of us can become overwhelmed by the enormity of them. And that's part of the problem.

When problems are seen as monolithic and massive, our ability to address them is bounded by our ability to understand them. Let's look outside of the field of education an example. The causes of heart disease are well publicized. Some we can't change, given that age, race, gender, and heredity all contribute to risk. However, there are many factors including whether or not we smoke, what we eat and drink, our amount of physical activity, and how much stress we are under that we can control. Preventing heart disease appears to be governed by an equation where one can identify risk factors and then control behaviors to minimize potential negative outcomes. Yet, as we all know, it is not that simple. When faced with changing the way we work, what we eat and drink, and how much we exercise, it all seems too much at once. Furthermore, changing our lifestyle to avoid a potential future crisis lacks the appeal that eating dessert or watching the game instead of exercising has today.

When problems are complex, our frustration with them increases. As our frustration increases so does our sense of helplessness and inadequacy. When we feel helpless and inadequate we are less likely to even begin addressing what ails us. Oddly, the first step in addressing big problems is to stop seeing them as big. The second step is to start seeing them as comprised of smaller, more manageable, bits and pieces.

However, before we think about how we can break problems down into more manageable bits, it is important to examine the ways we look at the issues that plague us. Unless we are aware of our preconceptions of and our predispositions toward solving our problems we are likely to misstep or repeat past mistakes. An example will help to make this point clear.

Like many schools across the nation, Fostter High adopted block scheduling as a structure to increase teaching and learning time. Although teachers at Fostter were initially wary of the innovation, they eventually grew to like the ability to flexibly structure class time as well as the opportunity the less intense schedule allowed them to know their students better. Students claimed that the block allowed them "fewer things to worry about, like tests or big projects all due on the same day."

However, other evidence suggested that the project was going less well than was expected. Although in-service had been offered concerning teaching in the block, teachers usually taught two classes back to back or used the second half of the block as a study hall. It was rare to find teachers using the time to enhance students' learning by offering labs, increased discussion, or group projects. When students took a course in the fall and then did not take the second-level class until the following fall, retention suffered and reteaching cut into the advanced course's curriculum. This was especially true in mathematics and foreign language where students sometimes took as much as a full year "off" between scheduling courses. Finally, there were concerns for students with poor study habits, who appeared to struggle when they had been absent or fallen behind for other reasons.

When a group of parents, troubled by these concerns, approached Principal Jon Bothler to discuss considering returning to a more traditional schedule for "at least part of the day," they were rebuffed. Bothler argued that "a lot of time and effort was invested in making these changes and I can't turn back now." He went on to add, "Besides, the block has worked elsewhere, these just have to be growing pains, we're only in year three. I know we'll be able to do better in the future. We've weathered problems like this when we made other changes. Parents always get worried too soon." Eventually, Bothler quelled the parents' concern by stating that he would continue to study the issues and offer more in-service and instructional support to teachers in the coming year.

It is easy to read Jon Bothler's comments as that of a principal who was out of touch with his school or unwilling to take criticism when trouble arises. However, this was not the case at Fostter High. Bothler was well known in the community for his commitment to the school and the students who went there. He attended every sports event, theater production, and debate tournament. When changes to program or policy were developed, he carefully studied the issues involved and made informed choices. Bothler stood up for faculty and staff in the face of complaints and gently but firmly required corrective action when necessary.

However, in this case Bothler made the wrong call. Rather than admit that block scheduling wasn't working as anticipated, he dug his heals in and chose to stay the course. Additional in-service didn't dramatically change classroom practice nor were other issues ever fully addressed (although a policy was adopted that required freshman to take math both semesters). Five years after the adoption, Bothler left for another position. In the face of complaints from parents, the school returned to a traditional seven-period schedule the following year.

So what happened here? Why was Bothler unable to clearly identify the problems involved with the implementation of block scheduling and address them? Why weren't the additional in-service and policy changes an adequate remedy? After all he was committed to the project, involved with matters that were important to the school's success, and working hard to implement a best practice. By all accounts his actions should have produced results. And that's the rub, because the problem was not with Bothler's actions. The problem was in how he *viewed the circumstances* that faced him.

As Bothler looked to the past for answers, he became trapped by his *problem-solving predispositions and preconceptions* of the issues. His predisposition toward in-service and policy development channeled his energy toward more of the same. Therefore, the answer to instructional problems was more in-service and the answer to student course-content retention was policy development. Bothler's preconceptions of parents and students limited his ability to notice salient differences in the problems he was facing with the block. Furthermore, his investment in the project was already quite high and pulling back seemed too costly.

When we think of these issues together we can see that Bothler made several common problem-solving errors. These include:

- commitment to practices and policies and sunken costs that seem too high to ignore,
- attribution errors that overlook contradictory evidence, and
- mislabeling and misdiagnosing problems.

By examining each of these ideas more fully we can see where Bothler went wrong and how you can avoid similar mistakes.

Commitment and Sunken Costs

Generally, we think of commitment as a good thing. As discussed in chapter 2, commitment has the potential to enhance our dedication to the task at hand. However, we can become overly committed as well. When this occurs it is difficult to let go of our position or choices even when they aren't working. We have all experienced this phenomenon. After paying fifty or seventy-five dollars to go to a play, we won't walk out even if we don't like it. Once we have paid for expensive repairs to an aging vehicle, it is hard to trade it in for the pittance the dealer is offering us. When we publicly claim we know where we are going, we'll refuse to stop and ask for directions.

So why do we do this? We hang on because we believe that our sunk costs are too high to let go. In some cases, sunk costs are real financial costs. When we've paid for the theater ticket or invested thousands in car repairs the monetary loss is real. It is hard to think that our hard-earned cash might have been wasted. In some cases, sunk costs are emotional. When we believe our judgment or pride is on the line, it is hard to admit we might be wrong. As difficult as losing or admitting we're wrong is, even more damage can be done when we hang on to ideas and choices long past their utility.

When we rely on "the way we've always done it" or when we dig our heels in and bluntly (or metaphorically) claim, "Because I said so," overcommitment and the sunk-cost effect is at play. When we find ourselves arguing for something long past the time everyone else has given up or justifying our choices to any and all that will listen, overcommitment and the sunk-cost effect may well be present. We don't like to lose or be wrong. However, in problem solving, knowing when to cut your losses is a good thing. Cutting your losses doesn't necessarily mean that you throw the towel in at the first sign of something going wrong. It does mean that when issues arise it is necessary to recognize them and work to remedy the problem rather than denying its existence or wishing it would go away.

Attribution Errors

Ask someone what his or her house is worth and they'll name you a price. Ask some who is wanting to buy that same house and they'll usually name you a lower price. In part, this is because we all want a good deal but it is also because we all perceive value based on qualities other than objective data. One person's beloved faux-finished dining room is a reminder of a favorite café in Paris; to a new buyer it might just be an eyesore. Objectively, what the dining room is worth is based on square footage and comparable houses in the neighborhood. Subjectively, the owner and the buyer each attribute a different value to the dining room because they look at it from different viewpoints.

In problem solving our reasoning is often no different. We attribute value to the innovations we wish to adopt, based on *where they have been successful* in the past and *who endorses* them. If a well-respected high school in the area adopts block scheduling other area high schools are more likely to do so. If the superintendent suggests we consider a new science series we are more likely to look into it than if a parent drops by with the recommendation. And sometimes we're wrong. Just because block scheduling works in another setting doesn't mean it is the best solution for your school. Just because a parent makes an observation or recommendation doesn't mean it isn't worth consideration.

When we make attribution errors they are often the fault of poor initial assessments. While misjudging a situation is not fatal in and of itself, the problem comes when we're faced with dealing with the concerns and issues that arise. We rarely go back and question our initial attributions. We assume that our choice to adopt block scheduling was a good one because we attribute the success of another school to the schedule. We assume that we were correct in rejecting a parent's assessment of a problem because, well, what do they really know about schools? In the end, the value we attribute to something becomes a set point, and we don't even think to question it.

Furthermore, we tend to value information that fits the answer we are looking to find. When we search for evidence that supports the answer we'd like, rather than the answer that might provide the best solution to a given problem, we can attribute value incorrectly. When we incorrectly attribute value our efficacy is decreased. In problem solving, rethinking past attributions might help you to see what is wrong in the present.

Mislabeling and Misdiagnosing Problems

Finally, sometimes we just miss the mark entirely. Bombarded with incredible amounts of information every day, we make sense of the world around us by sorting and classing that which confronts us into easily identifiable categories. Once we have placed a label on an issue (or person), it is hard to remove it. The label comes to define the issue to the exclusion of other equally plausible explanations.

In this way, we constrain our problem-solving choices. Student disruption, for example, is an issue in most schools. We care about student disruption because it gets in the way of student learning. However, student disruption can be considered a classroom management problem or an instructional problem. If we label it a classroom management problem, we are more likely to develop responses that address what students are able (and not able) to do and less likely to consider responses that focus on teaching behaviors. If we label student disruption as an instructional issue we are more likely to focus attention on how teachers engage students in classroom activity and less likely to employ student behavior reward systems.

When we misdiagnose problems we end up "solving" the wrong problem. When we solve the wrong problem our solutions are rarely effective because they aren't aligned with the issues we set out to address in the first place. If student disruption is a function of poor classroom instruction, all the rewards and sanctions in the world won't fix the real problem. On the surface, kids may well be better behaved but they won't be learning more.

By being aware of the preconceptions of and our predispositions toward the problems we face we are more likely to be able to reconsider our choices and make course corrections along the way. When we are able to reflect and see that we are defending sunken costs or have made an attribution error we are better able to regroup and recover. When we label our problems accurately we are more likely to expend our effort in ways that will produce the results we are seeking. By recognizing the ways we can incorrectly identify our problems we are better able to understand how to do it more successfully.

IDENTIFYING PROBLEMS—COMPLEXITY AND SMALL WINS

So let's return to the idea of breaking big problems into smaller units. When we break problems down into smaller units we benefit in two ways. First, we can *understand the complexities of our problems* more easily. Second, we can make progress by identifying *small wins*.

Understanding Complexity

Complexity comes to us in two forms—detail complexity and dynamic complexity. Detail complexity is just what it sounds like—managing the details of the day-to-day work of schools and schooling. Detail complexity includes tasks that, although time consuming, are fairly discrete. Distributing texts and materials, developing a schedule, and organizing assemblies and field trips are all examples of tasks that require detail complexity. You may have to sit down and think though the steps and processes you are going to use to complete the task, but in the end it is easily understood and accomplished. Stated as an equation, detail complexity suggests that if A occurs B will predictably follow.

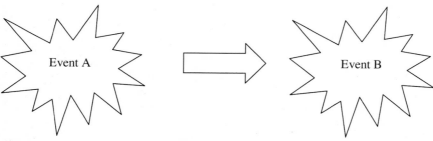

Figure 3.1. Detail complexity.

Dynamic complexity is more nuanced. Dynamic complexity requires that we consider the multiple forces at play in any situation or problem. Changing existing systems and structures, creating new policies and practices, and developing the school capacity to realize the promise of new ideas are all examples of the way dynamic complexity is present in schools. Dynamic complexity requires that we think about the process and that we also consider the multiple factors at play in any situation. If the equation for detail complexity is if A then B, the equation for dynamic complexity might be if A then B and C and D.

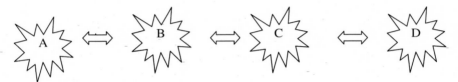

Figure 3.2. Dynamic complexity.

Currently, a popular strategy for addressing dynamic complex problems is root cause analysis (Andersen and Fagerhaug 2006). Root cause analysis suggests that by probing a problem for the reason it is occurring and then addressing the identified cause can assist us in solving our problems. In root cause analysis, instead of suggesting starting with the cause and seeking the effect (A $\rightarrow$ B), we often start with the effect (D) and look back over the events that might have gotten us there. In effect, the equation works backwards, where the presence of D suggests that C and B have interceded and caused the outcome (A). The difference is that rather than looking forward and anticipating what might occur, we look back for how we arrived where we are now.

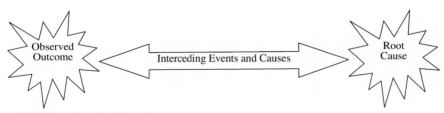

Figure 3.3. Root cause analysis.

Let's look at how this might work. Imagine that your car has been occasionally emitting an odd noise when you start it up. As the car warms up, the noise dissipates. Although ordinarily you would jump right on this and take the car into your mechanic, it is a busy time of the year and you choose to ignore the issue. You do note that over time the noise does appear to be occurring more often, lasting longer, and is perhaps a bit louder. Still, it does not appear to be causing other issues so it is easy to forget about. Then one day the noise is accompanied by a shudder, which also goes away almost immediately. The next week you are forced to admit that that you now have an almost constant whining noise while driving, a shudder when you start the car, and every time you accelerate, the car seems to hesitate. You decide that now is the time to see the mechanic. As you describe the issues that are wrong with the car, the mechanic asks a few questions and completes a root cause analysis this way:

- D (The problem): Hesitation upon acceleration, shudder at ignition, and constant engine noise.
- C (Likely cause): A failing fuel pump or the catalytic converter.
- B (Likely cause): A check of the records suggests that a recent service appointment has been missed.
- A (Root cause): Inattention to routine maintenance.

As annoying as car repairs are, figuring them out is usually a straightforward sequence of events. Noises can be reliably traced, parts replaced, and you are on your way. It may be expensive and you may wind up feeling foolish that you put aside routine maintenance, but nevertheless the cause-and-effect relationships are quite clear. The complexities of car repair might be complicated but they are (in most cases) direct and connected.

Locating root causes in educational dilemmas is less easy. Often the linkages are not clear and a multitude of *mediating and interacting variables* may cloud causal relationships. Let's examine both of these forms of dynamic complexity.

When mediating and interacting variables are at play, something gets in the way of or contributes to the expected end result. For example, on the day you have promised to read to a group of first graders, as soon as they all get settled in to hear your story, a fire truck pulls up in front of the school. No matter how hard you work to engage the students, the class probably will not be paying close attention. The presence of the fire truck is just too great of a distraction. It won't matter if you use funny voices, reorient your place in the room, or offer cookies as you read, the impulse to stare out the window will be too great. The fire truck will *mediate* your ability to capture the class's attention for the story.

Similarly, student performance is influenced by any number of variables. As the researchers of high stakes testing will agree, scoring well is influenced by economic and social factors as well as factors related to teacher experience and teaching methods and resources. All these influences *interact* and in turn, shape student results. In this way, teasing out which influence contributes the greatest effect can be tricky.

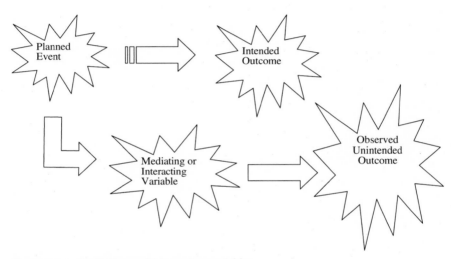

Figure 3.4.   Mediating and interacting variables.

Unintended Consequences

Finally, as we attempt to fix an issue in one area, our tinkering can cause consequences for other parts of the system. Unintended consequences occur when we fail to realize how intentions and outcomes are related through mediating and interacting variables. When we shift considerable amounts of our attention and time to the issues of the primary grades only to notice an increase of concerns at the secondary level a few months later, we suffer the unintended consequences of our inattention. The mediating variable in this case was, of course, the time and attention we usually pay to secondary education. The interacting variables may have included a lack of experienced teachers in key roles, a basketball team that made the playoffs requiring the principal to be away from the building, or the implementation of a new dress code policy.

We cannot always know, control, or predict the multiple factors that surround the problems we face. Because we cannot easily trace the causes of educational problems does not mean we should give up trying. Instead, we must be aware of how dynamic complexity influences our problem identification process.

For any given problem, dynamic complexity is a factor we must consider. The choices we make depend not only on what we see, but also on our ability to connect the dots in our search for a coherent story line. Undeniably, the exploration of these issues complicates our thinking about the problem identification process. At the same time, however, awareness of these issues should not lead you to lose your problem-solving resolve. Instead, by realizing big problems are often the results of smaller more dynamic complexities we can begin to think about the contributing factors of any problem and seek to identify and resolve each in turn.

Small Wins

Although many authors have written about the concept of small wins, the idea is most often credited to John Kotter (1999). He describes small wins as having three characteristics:

- There are visible signs that progress is being made.
- They are unambiguous; few will disagree that they represent positive change.
- They are clearly related to the change effort and cannot be easily credited to other factors.

Small wins help us to address big problems because they allow us to identify and solve issues incrementally by setting short-tem goals. When short-term problem-solving goals are in place, we are able to celebrate progress, allowing us to intensify effort and energy for future work. As we complete each short-term goal we can celebrate a small win. In this way, small wins are the building blocks of long-term accomplishments.

Let's look at this in practice. Imagine you are in the process of renovating your home. If you define success as having replaced the kitchen and bathroom cabinets and counters, installed new appliances, painted the entire interior, recarpeted all the bedrooms, refinished the basement, and completed installation of energy-efficient windows and siding, success is going to be a long time coming. On the other hand, if you break those projects up into smaller sequential units you can celebrate your new kitchen while contemplating new carpet colors.

Problems in schools can be similarly unpacked. Let's say you are troubled by a lack of student connection with the school. This problem might be broken down into these component parts:

- Student behaviors and actions.
  - How are they demonstrating a lack of interest?
- Openness of the adults in the school to student issues and concerns.
  - Is the school perceived as a warm and caring place?
- Programs to develop engagement with the school.
  - What does the school offer to interest students in coming?

You might then take on one of these areas starting with shadowing a student for a day or more to gain insight into their experience of the school. You might develop a survey for staff and faculty, students and parents to collect data concerning their sense of connection with the school. You could follow up those efforts by bringing a group of students, parents, and teachers together to discuss the issue (and perhaps the data collected) to hear how they think about the issue. By doing so, the problem can be identified and named. By developing understanding of the issue you can celebrate a small win because problems we understand are problems we are better able to solve.

Focusing on small wins allows us to *work within our bounds* of energy and resources and *manage the stress* of change. By scaling down our problems into manageable units we are more likely to remain committed to our projects and correct our direction when unexpected events occur. By doing less, we complete more.

Working Within Our Bounds

As people work to identify problems in schools it is easy to become overwhelmed by the scale of the effort. Since smaller projects are simpler in nature they are more easily understood, easier to organize and monitor. When people work on smaller projects, there is less required to complete each task and tasks will more easily fit into already crowded workdays. Working within smaller units allows us to practice new leadership behaviors and skills, thus, as we change, the people around us are given time to adjust to new ways of doing things. When the scale is reduced, feedback is more immediate and small mistakes are easily noticed and corrected. The resulting changes are more readily absorbed into the existing school culture allowing us to capitalize on them as we move to the next problem-identification cycle.

Managing the Stress of Change

Focusing on small wins allows us to reduce stress in three areas. Since changes are smaller they are less important and people are more likely to agree to be willing to try new ideas (Is that all you want?). Since tasks are more easily completed, demands are less challenging and we are more willing to commit to participation (If it's only one meeting . . .). Finally, since small wins do not require wholesale reform they capitalize on what we already know or can easily learn in a short time (I already know how to do that! or That's not that hard to learn!). As we reduce the stress of our efforts and turn our projects into smaller connected pieces, we are more able to manage the emotions of and build on our confidence in our abilities to change.

In summary, our ability to identify problems is less about listing everything we think is wrong with the school (although we do need to do some of that) and more about how we address the issues that face us. By knowing the biases we bring into the problem identification process, along with how to manage complexity and recognize smaller pieces of big issues we can be more effective. In the next section of this chapter, we will turn to looking at how we initiate actions to tackle the problems as we identify them.

INITIATING ACTIONS

It is only reasonable that once you have identified an issue of concern you would want to do something to remedy the problem. When we seek remedies for the problems that face us, we must consider a variety of possible actions and decide on the choice that is best suited to the issue at hand. The act of choosing between possible alternative actions is known as decision making. *Decision making asks us to make a conscious choice between two or more competing alternatives.* Decision theory suggests that for any given decision we can identify our possible actions, evaluate our choices, and select the solution from among the alternatives. Simple, right?

Not so fast. Unfortunately, decision making is not the rational, linear process that logical thinking would have us believe. Most decision-making models make a variety of problematic assumptions. These include the assumption that we know:

• what we want,
• exactly what is being decided,
• what is possible, and
• the costs involved with each possible choice.

Interestingly, when we approach the decision-making process we often think we know these answers. Our thinking goes something like this:

- What we want—We want students to learn more and we want to know how much they have learned.
- What is being decided—We are choosing how to go about implementing common assessments for our core subject classes.
- What is possible—We think that we can get draft assessments written within the first semester and piloted during the second.
- The costs involved—We will need to provide some in-service, in-writing common assessments, some planning time to get them written, and a system to easily score the exams and collect the results.

However, *decision making occurs in a context*. And no two contexts are the same. Sure, the physical context in which we work rarely changes. Yet, the specifics of each decision-making action are unique.

If the common assessment, decision-making process described above occurs just after a well-publicized district effort to encourage teachers to assess students in a consistent fashion, it will be received far differently than if it is simply announced at a faculty meeting. Similarly, if the staff participated in the decision to adopt common assessments, initiating the process will be quite different than if this decision was administrative in nature. If a good deal of trust already exists among the faculty, the writing process will run more smoothly than if the teachers in your school are known for their animosity toward each other. If it takes the algebra teachers the same amount of time it takes the English department to develop the common assessment, your timeline will not be disrupted. And so on. . . .

In other words, initiating actions that are designed to dispel problems requires that we pay attention to the context of the school. When we pay attention to the context of our school our problem-solving efforts can be more successful. Context includes the people with whom we work, the time we have for addressing a problem, how we choose to invest our effort, and the ways we define the targets for and the outcomes we seek. When we think about initiating actions in this manner, effective problem solving requires that we consider the following:

- How we will *intensify leadership efforts* across the school to include others in the problem-solving process.
- Over what *period of time* we expect the process to occur.
- Where we will *target our efforts* and who they will involve.
- What the *expected outcomes* of our efforts will include.

- The ways we will go about *strategically implementing actions* required to get where you want to go.

Intensifying Leadership Effort

Intensified leadership assumes that *there is deliberately broadened meaningful involvement* of teachers, parents, and (as appropriate) students and/or community members in the problem-solving process (Kruse and Louis 2009). By deepening *collective responsibility* for finding and solving problems, people become more accountable for meshing the larger goals and vision of the school with their motivations for being there. When we include others in our problem-solving practice we increase our ability to understand the problems we face as well as enhance our chances of finding a solution that will be mutually acceptable.

Intensified leadership opens the boundaries of problem solving to include a wide variety of members of the school community in new roles, and it asks them to become involved in generating new kinds of decisions and practices. Intensified leadership suggests that when organizational members work in concert with each other they are able to bring together their individual knowledge and expertise. In turn, when individual knowledge and expertise are combined, better outcomes are possible for the school. As the age-old adage notes, *people will support that which they help to create.* When people are included in the process of choosing and developing the actions to be implemented they are more likely to support the effort and be invested in the success of the project.

Timing and Timelines

Another contextual variable we must consider is time. Our culture is replete with proverbs about time. Time is money. Haste makes waste. Time flies when you're having fun. Patience is a virtue. The early bird gets the worm. Or in its more modern cynical form, the early bird gets the worm, but the second mouse gets the cheese. It is hard to miss the message that time and timing matter. The proverbs and our past experience with the constraints of time suggest that expedience matters, as does the amount of consideration we have given our choices. Furthermore, how we experience the pressures of time is evidenced in our emotions. Our emotional state—calm detachment or hotheaded fervor—telegraphs our indifference to or investment in the issues we currently face.

The amount of time we invest in a decision matters. Likewise, when we choose to act also matters. Haste tends to lead to poor decision choices. When we choose quickly we often do not wait to collect enough data to inform our decision choices. Procrastination often leads to lost opportunity. When we fail to make decisions in a timely fashion we may miss possibilities that could lead to positive outcomes for our students. The issue is *consideration and balance*. When we initiate actions in regard to solving problems, time must be considered. Initiatives that are introduced in May have little chance of success; likewise complex initiatives that are months in the planning stage often cannot be reasonably executed in a few weeks. Considering the calendar, other important tasks and responsibilities as well as the skill set of those involved in the activity can help to breed success.

Balance is important as well. Not asking too much at any one time allows for organizational members to focus on critical matters and complete tasks with ease and insight. When people are provided a reasonable yet significant amount of time to incorporate changes into their daily patterns and actions, new ideas are more likely to take root. In this way, attending to time as part of your process of initiating actions can, in the long run, help to assure acceptance and goal attainment.

Targeted Effort

As if the pressures of time were not stressful enough, school leaders often feel overwhelmed by the amount of work they are expected to accomplish. The daily management tasks of the district and school seem overwhelming and leaders report that they have little time for substantive work. With alarming regularity, schools are showered with uncoordinated innovations, adoptions, and programs, and overburdened improvement agendas. When there are too many initiatives, priorities are unclear. When priorities are unclear it is difficult to know where to invest our effort.

Unlike strategic planning efforts that focus attention on broad, long-term goals, targeting efforts suggests that working through the problem-solving cycle includes focusing on smaller coordinated units of change. Approaching tasks as a series of *coordinated responses* allows leaders the opportunity to engage in more unified problem-solving practices. In turn, these smaller units of targeted effort contribute to and result in larger purposeful actions. Within the day-to-day experiences of teachers and students such actions are experienced as predictable and understandable within the context of the school's goals. Consequently, the leader can make the most of his or her efforts and at the same time develop trust and respect among faculty, staff, and the community.

Expected Outcomes

If you expect people to follow your lead, it is important that they know where they are headed. Furthermore, people are more likely to follow you if you are honest and open about the journey. No one expects things to run smoothly all of the time. Bumps in the road offer us opportunity for new insights and understandings. On the other hand, people are likely to lose confidence in a leader who consistently manages actions poorly. The key is to maintain equilibrium between navigating minor course adjustments and requiring wholesale revisions of schedules and plans. When we are focused on and clear about our intentions, this is a far easier task.

Providing a clear sense of where you are headed is vital. Turning expected outcomes into targeted goal statements can provide direction for your problem-solving actions. All too often we state our outcome goals too broadly, for example, "We will do better next year." At other times we state outcome measures that are unreasonable, for example failing schools will often set achievement goals that would require a 500 percent improvement over a three-year period. When we set unattainable expectations or fail to define our goals clearly, we can confuse faculty and staff, parents and students instead of motivating them.

When we are clear about the outcomes we expect to achieve and state those goals as attainable measurable performances, we are more likely to remain on course. Clear measurable performance goals provide followers certainty that their efforts are worthwhile and encourage participation by making clear what is expected of all members. Clear, measurable, realistic performance goals contain statements that:

- state what is to be accomplished,
- contain a deadline for achievement or review, and
- demonstrably link new actions to prior efforts and outcomes.

Strategic Implementation of Activities

If a leader takes the contextual variables of time, effort, and outcome seriously, his or her actions can be more strategic. Being strategic suggests that you consider the issues discussed above and thoughtfully address each. Thoughtful attention to the following matters increases the potential for effective successful problem-solving efforts:

People

Including others lightens your load and increases investment in the choices that are made. However, whom you include, and the role you ask them to play, makes the difference between a smoothly operating committee and a group mired in disagreement and strife. There are several ways to formulate your team; you might include a small trusted collection of teachers, a larger group of more opinionated parents, or a mix of community and staff and faculty. Whatever configuration you decide upon, it is important that people are chosen carefully and strategically. Representation matters as well. If the issue primarily concerns middle school students, it makes sense to include middle school-level teachers and parents (and perhaps students) in your thinking. If the issue concerns the whole school, you would want a broader group's input.

Finally, clarifying the role members are to play at the start of the committee assures that people know what is expected of them. If the group's role is fact finding, people should know that they would not have decision-making authority. Similarly, if the group will be responsible for disseminating information and supporting the project, people should know that their commitment includes assistance in these areas. It might be helpful to include a dissenter or devil's advocate in the group as well. Real dialogue about change efforts must address the negative as well as the positive. Finding someone willing to raise the hard questions during the planning stages can preclude opposition later in the effort.

In short, when inviting people to work on a problem-solving effort you must consider:

- who you will include,
- why you are including these people and not others,
- the role they will play,
- the amount of decision-making power the group will enjoy, and
- the tangible outcome the group will provide.

Time

Strategic action includes setting a clear timeline for the problem-solving effort. You may create a timeline prior to beginning the effort or complete the timeline as part of the early stages of initiating action. In either case, timelines should include attention to how much time is needed to plan for, learn about, inform others, implement ideas and actions, and evaluate results. Timelines can be ample or pragmatic. That is, they may allow the team as long as necessary to complete the work or they may set an aggressive end point with due dates along the way. Dependent on the context of your decision, the kind of timeline you choose can determine your results.

Ample timelines allow people plenty of time to read, learn, and discuss pending issues. When a great deal of learning is required ample timelines allow members the opportunity to reflectively consider new ideas and synthesize their learning. More leisurely in nature, without careful monitoring, ample timelines can encourage procrastination. On the other hand, if you can enjoy the opportunity to dream, at least for a bit, ample timelines can create idyllic memories and develop deep-rooted trust among and between faculty and staff.

Pragmatic timelines are more common. Pragmatic timelines assert themselves requiring that members roll up their sleeves and get to work. More focused in nature, they allow little time for dreaming and encourage decisive action. Pragmatic timelines produce work in short order and rely on a leader's responsiveness and competence. When thinking about time, you should consider:

- how quickly results are required;
- how much new learning is required to solve the problem;
- how long it will take to inform others of new ideas, decisions, or changes;
- how long it will take to implement the plan, policy, or practice; and
- how soon you can determine if the expected results are being achieved.

Costs

Any project has costs. Some are tangible and include materials, in-service and workshop attendance, or teacher stipends. Process costs are subtler and include expenditures of good faith and will, trust and respect, or time and effort. In most cases both forms of costs are at play. In most contexts, our resources are limited and we are usually restricted by how much we (and others) are willing to expend in any given effort.

Completing a cost-benefit analysis can be useful in determining if a project is worth the money and effort invested. Cost-benefit analysis weighs the total costs of a project against the potential outcomes of completion. In business this is somewhat more easily accomplished. A company might compute the cost of a new operation, add in training and downtime, and balance that against projected revenues. Because many of these costs are known, the calculus of the decision is more simply determined.

In education we can often compute the costs of the inputs—usually training and materials—however, computation of the outputs—most often measured as increased learning—is less immediate and tangible. While it is important for any leader to consider process costs, the lack of immediate and tangible outcomes makes it a paramount concern for school leaders. When times are good, well-executed problem-solving efforts can contribute to your reputation. However, placing your name, the hard earned trust of your community and faculty, or your social and political capital on the line should be something you do knowingly rather than be a casualty of poor planning.

Prior to embarking on any project it is important that leaders determine the costs involved and make plans to address limitations and contain costs. Concerns related to costs include:

- the tangible expenses involved with this project and
- the potential wins for and losses to your reputation.

EVALUATING RESULTS

We would like to believe that after taking the time and effort to make a good decision our work is over. And in many schools it is. Curricular reforms are initiated, only to be abandoned a few weeks or months later. New policies are designed but never fully implemented. After starting a project, only a few committed teachers retain innovative practices. Worse yet, no one seems to notice—or care. Inevitably, the new policy or practice is deemed a failure and the school moves on to try yet another innovation. And the cycle repeats itself.

Schools adopt, design, and implement new ideas only to have them wither and die and, in turn, adopt, design, and implement more new ideas that one by one, wither and die. Sadly, enduring problems do not get solved. Why does this happen? Why do otherwise smart, committed people get stuck trying to solve the same problem over and over again? Are school leaders miserable decision makers? When faced with a variety of alternatives do they simply (and repeatedly) choose the wrong one? In most cases, no.

Simply put, *the failure of many problem-solving efforts is not caused by poor decisions*. Rather, it is caused by *inadequate and incomplete evaluation* after the decision has been made. It is not enough to choose wisely and then hope for the best.

Effective problem solving requires that we evaluate the results of our actions as a regular and consistent part of our work. Evaluating results means that we pay attention to the ways our decisions are helping us to meet our goals, teach us about our school and the students in it, and affect the school's culture and climate. Although the coming chapters will specifically take on the ways you can establish systems and structures that can aid you in evaluating your results a few general ideas will be offered here.

Our attentions must be directed toward:

- goal attainment including measures progress and areas of need and
- learning from this problem-solving cycle and implementing what we have learned in new problem-solving situations.

Measures of Progress and Areas of Need

School leaders often wait for the June arrival of test results before they begin the evaluation cycle. They reason that absent hard data concerning how students are learning they cannot draw valid conclusions about an innovation's worth. However, in most cases, this is too late. When we wait too long to make corrections we:

- lose momentum,
- risk missteps and errors, and
- fail to recognize how successful practice can become established in our school.

To be effective, our actions must be evaluated throughout the problem-solving cycle. Data evaluating how an innovation or idea is received must be collected and taken seriously so that concerns are addressed along the way. Teachers, parents, and students can identify if learning is engaging. Faculty and staff can report if they are using the materials as they were intended. Classroom assessments can provide measures of where the materials are adequate to meet student needs and where gaps are present. Others can help us understand how innovations are helping us achieve our goals and where they fall short. We can make mid-term corrections as needed, providing mentoring and coaching as necessary for teachers and tutoring and enrichment for students. In this way, ongoing and regular monitoring of the implementation of our actions can help assure we attain our goals.

Learning in the Problem-Solving Process

Part of the evaluation process is learning from and about our efforts. To learn from our actions it is important that we step back and look at the ways new ideas enhance or challenge the existing structures and belief systems within the school. To learn we must seek out our errors in logic and action and work to correct them. We can do this by working within the systems and structures we currently understand and find comfortable. Or we can step outside those structures and systems and look more broadly at the issues in our schools and realize that potentially the norms and values of the school contribute to our most problematic issues.

When we engage in efforts to correct errors by relying on improving the technical aspects of the system we focus our efforts narrowly. At times such close scrutiny is needed. Technical systems fail. We forget to include minor issues of policy in student handbooks or a tweak of the schedule makes the hallways less crowded. We can learn from solving these problems that attention to detail matters. But when you've tweaked and changed and reformed and reassessed and the issue still remains problematic, it is probably necessary to step back and look more broadly.

By looking at the school as a whole we can often see that the enduring dilemmas we face cannot be solved by simple technical solutions. Instead we need to reflect more generally on the situations that face us and learn our way into understanding them. In other words we need to learn to view the problems we face differently so that we can employ different solutions for solving them. As we evaluate the results of our actions we can learn how to think about our schools differently. By learning how we learn, future problem-solving efforts can run more smoothly and successfully.

COMPLETING THE CYCLE

This chapter began with the quote, "We are too busy mopping the floor to turn off the faucet." Poorly executed problem solving is a lot like floor mopping. We spend our time cleaning up problems rather than locating the source of our troubles and tackling the causes of our problems. By attending to the *tasks* of problem solving—identifying problems, initiating actions, and evaluating results—school leaders can locate and turn off the faucet. Ensuring against leaks requires that we develop systems and structures, policies and practices and communicate our intentions clearly. Learning how to effectively do this *work* increases the abilities of school leaders to solve problems. We will now turn to learning how this can happen in your school.

KEY POINTS

- Leadership is comprised of behaviors and activities that provide a variety of arenas in which problem solving may occur. The challenge for leaders is to capitalize on circumstances that present themselves and use those to enhance school improvement efforts.
- Identifying problems requires us to avoid overcommitment, sunk costs, attribution errors, and misdiagnosis.
- Initiating problem-solving actions is more than decision making. Initiating action requires that we look more broadly at the context of the school and intensify leadership efforts, consider the time it will take to make and

implement actions, intentionally target effort, identify expected outcomes, and strategically implement problem-solving work.
- Evaluating results requires that leaders follow through by monitoring problem-solving efforts. By monitoring problem-solving efforts, leaders can learn how goals are being met and how they can learn to better solve future problems.

CHAPTER REFLECTIONS

1. In what ways can you take advantage of the chances that present themselves in your school?
2. What problem-solving predispositions and preconceptions do you bring to your work? How might examining those change the way you view your school?
3. How can you intensify problem-solving leadership in your school?
4. How does time play a role in your school? Are there ways to restructure your time? How might changing how you spend your time make a difference in your problem-solving efforts?
5. What are the costs of your current problems? Which ones are tangible? Which ones have more to do with trust, respect, and reputation?
6. How do you currently evaluate the results of your problem-solving efforts? What might you change about your actions to make evaluation a larger part of your problem solving?

CHAPTER ACTIVITIES

You can practice the ways the problem-solving cycle can play out in your school by completing these four activities.

Activity 1: Assess Your Own Behaviors and Activities

Using the chart below, list the five tasks or activities on which you spend your most time. Identify the leadership behaviors exercised in the completion of those tasks.

Leadership Behaviors	Leadership Activity				
	Task 1	Task 2	Task 3	Task 4	Task 5
Communicating purpose, vision, and goals					
Providing encouragement and recognition					
Establishing rapport, trust, and respect Obtaining resources					
Adapting procedures or policies					
Monitoring improvement efforts					
Managing student behavior					

Reflect on the questions listed below.

- What leadership behaviors are addressed in your top five tasks?
- What do the results say about how you use your time?
- Is there a balance of effort and energy?
- Do other leaders in your school or district use their time in similar ways?
- What do the results say about the kinds of problems you are able to proactively address?
- What kinds of problems are you most likely to miss?
- How might you think about your work differently?
- What might be the outcome of thinking about your work in this way?

Activity 2: Identifying Problems in Your School

This exercise begins with brainstorming a list of problems in your school that are worthy of your attention. Try to keep the list focused on issues that have the potential to affect real change and issues that you can reasonably address (for example, listing an old building as the cause of all your problems might be real but it is probably not something you have control over). Once the list is completed, choose the top five priorities.

Priority list:
1. _____
2. _____
3. _____
4. _____
5. _____

Take each of the priority areas and search for contributing factors or potential causes, mediating and interacting variables that might be interfering with resolving the issue.

List those here:

Priority Issue: _____		
Contributing factors	*Mediating Variables*	*Interacting Variables*

Reflection:

- In what ways does this make your problem clearer?
- Have you identified contributing factors, mediating and interacting variables that surprise you?

- Identify the contributing factors, mediating and interacting variables that relate to each other. Link those by arrows. How do these issues stand in the way of problem-solving efforts?
- Would other members of the school view this issue the same way?
- How might their viewpoints be different?
- Can the priority issue be broken up into smaller parts?
- What might those parts look like?
- Where might you be able to identify one or more areas as a small win?
- How might you go about obtaining a small win on this issue immediately?

Activity 3: Initiating Actions in Your School: A Planning Guide

Choose an action you wish to implement in your school. Answer the following questions to assist you in planning your actions and efforts:

- What problem do you want to address?
  - Is it a core issue of concern?
  - Will addressing this problem make other issues within the school easier?
  - How can addressing this problem help you build community and trust?
- What is the outcome you wish to achieve?
  - Where does this outcome fit with prior issues and efforts in your school?
  - What is reasonable to achieve in the time you have to complete the project?
- Where will you target your efforts?
  - Is this a schoolwide issue?
  - Is this an issue that only affects a portion of your school population?
  - Why is this a valuable target?
  - How will these efforts coordinate with other initiatives in your school?
- Who will you include in your planning and implementation team?
  - What roles will they play?
  - How will you use their knowledge and skills to assure success?
- How much time will it take to complete:
  - Planning?
  - Learning?
  - Informing others of the change?
  - Implementation?
  - Evaluation?
- What are the tangible and process costs involved with this effort?
  - Materials?
  - Time?
  - Trust and respect?
  - Reputation?

Activity 4: Evaluating Results in Your School

Do you evaluate results? Assess your orientation toward evaluating the outcomes of your problem-solving efforts.

After a new idea or practice is implemented in my school I...	Always	Sometimes	Never
Check in with teachers to see how it is working.	3	2	1
Check in with parents to see how it is working.	3	2	1
Check in with students to see how it is working.	3	2	1
Look for ways to problem solve a similar but new issue.	3	2	1
Devise and execute a plan to collect data to determine how well things are working.	3	2	1
Focus energy on working to be sure the idea or practice is implemented with fidelity.	3	2	1
Discuss my impressions of the project's success with others.	3	2	1
Discuss my impressions concerning remaining areas of need with others.	3	2	1
Convene one month, three month and six month reviews of the project.	3	2	1
Evaluate what I can learn from the implementation of this project to use in other new projects.	3	2	1
Accept that some ideas just don't work in my school.	3	2	1
Look at the ways this new idea has changed other practices or behaviors in my school for the better.	3	2	1
Look at the ways this new idea has created new problems in my school.	3	2	1
Celebrate the success of a project well done.	3	2	1
Identify and reward the efforts of others in making the project a success.	3	2	1

Column A + Column B + Column C =

- If your score is above 35, good going! It looks like you are well practiced at evaluating results and learning from your problem-solving efforts. Keep up the good work; you can enhance your efforts by including others in the process or by creating formal systems and structures to communicate your efforts.
- If your score is between 25 and 35, well done but could be better. Review the items you scored as a 1 or a 2 and think about ways you can increase the ways you follow through on and learn problem-solving efforts. Look to

ways to boost your efforts by developing formal systems and structures to increase reflection on progress and communication about results.

- If your score is between 15 and 25, you may be working hard, but probably your follow-up efforts need some attention. Look for ways to involve others in the process and how to be more consistent in your evaluation of efforts. Keeping a calendar or log devoted to evaluation efforts might help you to develop your practice and skill.

✑ THINKING ABOUT THE WORK OF PROBLEM SOLVING ✑

In the next three chapters we will explore the *work* school leaders do that sets the stage for effective problem solving. Like puzzle builders who employ strategic tactics to address the complexity of the puzzle at hand, each of the strategic areas of work provides school leaders the *tools to approach problem solving*. These tools include effective communication, supportive systems, and constructive policies and provide you with a variety of ways to tackle the problems you face. However, these tools are not meant to be separate strategies a leader employs and checks off his or her problem-solving list. Instead, these tools are to be used to support the problem-solving cycle introduced in chapter 3. In other words, as a school leader goes about the tasks of identifying problems, initiating actions, and evaluating results, he or she uses the tools of effective communication, constructive policy, and supportive systems to solve problems.

In this way, a leader might consider a communication strategy as a tool to approach the development of a new system or policy designed to address a problem. Similarly, the creation of a data collection system might foster conversation among teachers about how to evaluate student work. The resulting communication could then influence the development of a homework policy. As you can see, the potential permutations of how these tools might interact are many. We cannot possibly examine all of the ways these ideas can act together. Rather, the intention of the coming chapters is to provide a *foundational knowledge and skill set* designed to foster collaboration with others and enthusiasm for strategies that enhance problem-solving efforts.

Chapter Four

Effective Communication—Talking about Problem Solving

Good communication is as stimulating as black coffee, and just as hard to sleep after.

—Anne Morrow Lindbergh

The only way school leaders can make others aware of their intentions is to effectively communicate them. Effective communication relies on a leader's ability to clearly articulate goals and objectives and to do so in a manner that engages, rather than distances, others. In this chapter we will discover ways to enhance communication in schools and how effective communication stimulates problem-solving efforts.

In this chapter you will learn why:

- Strong communication skills enhance a leader's ability to convey goals and link words to actions.
- Negotiation and bargaining are important pieces in the problem-solving puzzle.
- Conveying difficult messages must be done with consistency and care.
- Effective communication helps to build a school culture that is open to problem-solving work.

THE IMPORTANCE OF COMMUNICATION

From our first cry at birth, we communicate our needs and wants. As we age, we become more adept at communicating with those about us. Our cries become words that then become phrases and sentences, conversations and arguments. Furthermore, with instruction and practice, we move beyond oral language and expand our communication to contain any number of written forms including the traditional—journals, letters, and papers—and the electronic—e-mail, text messages, and blogs. No matter if we are communicating in oral or written form, our ability to communicate allows us to *exchange messages* about matters important and mundane.

As we have all experienced, exchanging messages is not an easy task. Sometimes we are lucky and our messages are received well. Whomever we are speaking with understands what we meant to communicate and accepts our words. At other times we are not as lucky. We get misunderstood and our messages become distorted or confused. Sometimes the miscommunication is our own fault; we have misspoken before we could think about our words. At other times, the miscommunication is the fault of the receiver, who, upon receiving our message, twists our words into something we did not intend.

Communication, whether written or oral, is difficult because every message we send carries several messages encoded within it. At the core, lies the *factual message*. However, embedded within our words is often an *emotional message* concerning how we feel or wish others would feel about the current situation. *Who sends* the message also matters and the character or reputation of the speaker contributes to the worth of and response to the message. Finally, no matter the *intended meaning*, how our messages are received is out of our hands.

In this fashion, the same words—"I'm fine"—can have radically different meanings. "I'm fine" may mean you are, in fact, fine. The factual message suggests that nothing is wrong; you are well, not bothered by anything in particular, and not needing any assistance. However, "I'm fine" may not mean that at all. It may mean, "Ask me more." Or in the parlance of stereotypical guilt-inducing mothers everywhere, "I'm fine" can be an emotional hook used to engage an inattentive family in conversation or to coerce them into visiting just a little bit longer.

Because *communication is a transaction between two or more people*, how the message is decoded is dependent on who spoke and how the words were uttered. The words themselves have a factual meaning but *communicative meaning* can only be constructed when the emotional and personal context is understood. Consequently, meaning is developed through speaking, listening, and interpreting oral or written messages.

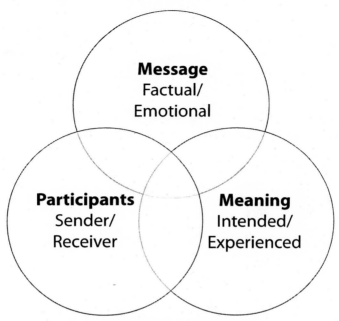

Figure 4.1.   Layers of communicative messaging.

Consider this simple interaction between a parent and a principal, in which the parent's message is, "My child needs extra time this week to complete his math homework." Dependent on how the parent phrases the request, the meaning of the message is altered. If an otherwise calm parent places her emphasis on the words "this week" you may attribute the request of more time to some special circumstance of this week's schedule. If the same parent places her emphasis on the words "math homework" you may attribute the request to the difficulty of the week's mathematics content.

If, from the tone of the spoken message, you assume the former, you might agree that an additional day is warranted. If the message's tone suggests the latter, you may suggest a visit to the math lab for tutoring to address the problem. If you read the verbal emphasis correctly, your response is likely to be greeted with gratitude. If you have the misfortunate to incorrectly read the intent behind the spoken words, the parent's demeanor may shift from calm to combative quite rapidly. Your ability to communicate effectively in this situation (as in others) rests on your ability to interpret the factual content within the emotional context of the message. Effective communicators consider the *content and contexts* of spoken and written messages.

Every day school leaders communicate with a variety of people including teachers, parents, students, and community members. Each hears our messages in the context of what is important to them. For example, teachers care about matters related to teaching and learning, curriculum and instruction, and the work required of them. Parents are interested in the safety and security, progress and achievement of their children. Students care about what is expected of them and how they are doing. Community members care about how money is spent and how the school contributes to the community's overall well-being.

Our communication with each must be factually consistent. We also need to emotionally connect with the needs of each group. This is not an easy task. However, it is possible. By knowing how to manage your communication you can improve your problem-solving success.

TALKING WITH OTHERS—COMMUNICATION'S ROLE IN PROBLEM SOLVING

The key to communicating with others is to *start by considering their experience*. This means asking questions and listening to the answers in an effort to understand their underlying concerns, interests, preferences, and needs. By knowing where they stand and what they want, you are more likely to solve the right problem and solve it on the first try. Let's look at an example.

Located in a semi-urban suburb, Johnsen Secondary School (JSS) was known for its innovative arts-centered curriculum. Unlike other neighborhood schools in the surrounding district, students were admitted to JSS only after auditioning in one of four program areas—music, theater, visual arts, or dance. Although the school was popular because of its arts program, it was also academically challenging.

However, JSS could not avoid being swept up in the district's concerns. Swayed by media attention to rising discipline problems, the school board decided to respond by reviewing the district's comprehensive discipline policy. One issue under review was the development of a districtwide uniform dress code. Many schools within the district had adopted uniforms and it was thought that a districtwide effort could unify the inconsistencies that resulted from a dozen separately crafted policies while still discouraging gang-related dress and encouraging an academic tone within the buildings.

One school that had not adopted any form of a dress code was JSS. As an arts school, parents and faculty had taken a more relaxed approach to student dress, embracing student dress as a form of self-expression. At first, parents and students believed that the new uniform policy would not apply to the school. However, as publicity for the policy increased, it become clear that the school board intended all students, no matter what school they attended, to adopt the new code.

A student protest was staged at JSS against the new policy. Tipped off by a parent, the protest received front-page coverage by the local media. In turn, counterprotests at other schools branded JSS students as "snobs." Tensions mounted. The board was split. Some board members supported taking a strong unbending stance and enforcing the uniform policy, claiming that they would look weak if they "played favorites" and exempted individual schools. Others suggested that perhaps some schools should be treated differently and that "equity rather than equality" was called for in this matter.

As you can imagine, the board wished they had started the revision of the discipline policy with a less divisive issue. However, since they wanted to solve the problem quickly and to find a mutually agreeable solution, they provided for an hour of public comment on the next board agenda. As was district custom, at the meeting parents, students, teachers, and administrators were each given three minutes to speak to the matter. During the presentations, a recorder took down the major points of each argument on large white boards. At the end of the hour, the board thanked the community for coming. They announced that they would consider the issues and make a decision within the month.

After the room had emptied, the board worked to understand the concerns of each faction. It soon became clear that several distinct tensions were present. Understandably, from the district's perspective, cohesion, consistency, and unity were all important and worthy values. From the JSS's perspective, autonomy, individualism, and distinctiveness set them apart from other schools and provided them an identity as members of the artistic community.

As the board deliberated they soon realized that the problem they faced was, on the surface, about the uniform dress code. Underneath lay a more perplexing matter. What the parents and students at Johnsen had argued was that they were unique. And they were right. They were unique because the school had been designed to be different from other schools in the district. Their purposeful uniqueness caused them to see the potential uniform policy differently than other schools. Rather than seeing themselves like everyone else,

Table 4.1.   Comparing District and School Values

District-Level Values	JSS (Building-Level) Values
Cohesion	Autonomy
Consistency	Individualism
Unity	Distinctiveness

they asserted their independence by creating and nurturing a school culture in which difference was valued and celebrated.

When the board viewed the issue from the JSS point of view they saw that the enforcement of a uniform policy conflicted with the school's understanding of the arts mission. Consequently, their resistance fit the school's avant-garde image. On the other hand, when viewed from another standpoint, JSS was "a school first." Thus, the uniform policy was appropriate. JSS's interest was to maintain their individuality. The district's interest was to create consistent policy.

Early on in the dispute, neither side saw the other's stance as reasonable. Each wanted to win. As each position was better understood, it became more possible to reach a satisfactory solution. The board conceded that consistency rather than uniformity was their goal and JSS accepted the fact that they could maintain their individuality and still be part of the larger district community. The solution? The district adopted a "standardized dress policy" that provided the broad outlines of acceptable clothing (collared shirts, no visible midriffs or overly short skirts, socks and close-toed shoes) instead of a uniform policy. The standardized dress policy provided the consistency the board wanted with enough space for the individualism JSS craved.

The result was a classic win-win solution. Each side got a solution they could live with, the negative publicity died down, and everyone felt understood. Interestingly, neither side got what they first thought they should. On the other hand, both sides were able to avoid the pain of a protracted battle. What made this problem-solving process different was communication. Once each perspective was clear, finding a satisfactory solution was only an Internet search away. Table 4.2 outlines the effective communication lessons that can be learned from this vignette.

NEGOTIATION AND BARGAINING

In education when we think about negotiations, the first thing that comes to mind is settling union contracts. Negotiations suggest a once-every-four-year cycle where we sit on opposite sides of the table and argue over salary and health benefits. Everything else school leaders do falls under some other euphemistic category of communication. We claim we discuss options, manage conflict, resolve disputes, or reconcile differences. If we are honest, we admit that we negotiate and bargain all the time.

Think about the problems you spend your time working on. They probably fall into one of these broad categories: student progress and achieve-

Table 4.2 Effective Communication Lessons

Effective Communication Lessons
Others don't see the world the way we do.
Others are governed by beliefs, values, motivations, and needs that are important to them.
Listening to and understanding others' needs and concerns is vital to creating a satisfactory solution.
Clarifying our own position allows us to understand what is important to us in the situation.
Finding a solution that is acceptable to all members of the situation is the goal.
Solution finding is the result of generating creative alternatives and testing the situational fit of each.
Change requires that the alternative be seen as less painful than the current circumstance or other potential futures.
Embracing a solution other than the one you originally wanted is not a loss, rather it is savvy problem solving.

ment; student behavior and discipline; faculty and staff behavior and discipline (called human resource management); building maintenance and community outreach and involvement. Although each of these areas requires a different foundation of understanding—progress and achievement involves managing data, human resource management entails employment law, outreach and involvement necessitates understanding the community that surrounds the school—each requires that *we work with and talk to people*.

Working with and talking to people involves a continual process of persuasion and influence, negotiation and bargaining to encourage others to agree with us. Whether it is a student who misbehaves in class or a faculty member who needs to leave a bit early to attend a graduate course every Wednesday, we strike deals about what we will do for them if they do something we would like. We solve our problems by giving a little and taking a little. The more effective we are at giving and taking, the more smoothly our schools operate.

As the well-known negotiator Herb Cohen (2003) notes, when we *negotiate* we engage in a *mutual discussion of and arrangement for the terms of a transaction or agreement*. Once we have decided on the terms of the agreement we make a *bargain* where both parties *agree to what they will do and promise to carry out* that to which they have agreed. Negotiation is the discussion; the bargain is the promised behaviors and outcomes. Once everyone fulfills his or her obligations, the result is a problem solved. Here's how it works.

SUCCESSFUL NEGOTIATING

The basis for all successful negotiations is to begin with a clear understanding of the issue. Since we have already discussed problem identification in some detail, we will not review those ideas. Suffice it to say that if you are not clear about what you are negotiating—whether it is the price on a new car or the concert band schedule—you are less likely to be successful.

One way to be sure you *understand the issue* is to frame it as a specific and shared problem. If framed as a mutual problem, people are more likely to agree to work with you to resolve the matter and to support the eventual solution. In this way, the concert band schedule is about creating an opportunity for students to learn performance skills and to showcase their hard work rather than a confrontation about equal performance time.

One reason we are sometimes distressed about the problems we are required to solve is that we accept the frame others place around them. When a teacher, parent, or student comes to you and says, "X is a problem," we usually move forward to solve X. How many times in your life have you been blindsided by accepting one view of the situation before considering others? Probably a lot.

It happened to me just last week. I'm on the board of my homeowners association and a neighbor approached the board with a property line dispute. Armed with plot maps, he successfully convinced us that a second neighbor had constructed a fence running the length of his property and "stealing 100 square feet of his land." Prompted by questions from him, our conversation then moved to a discussion of fence removal and the costs involved. The claim of one hundred stolen square feet was inflammatory and the maps were persuasive. For a short time, we allowed him to frame the conversation as one about "stolen" land and redress. Once we accepted his framing, we moved forward as if his facts were correct. Finally, we came to our senses, reframed the issue as a property line dispute, thanked him for his presentation, and expressed our desire to obtain a second survey of the property line.

When we take a minute and step back and evaluate if X is really a problem (or *the* problem) we can open new avenues for thinking about the issue. By accepting the frame others put on the facts, we limit our ways of thinking about those facts. It may take a bit more time to rethink the frames, but by reframing you may discover less inflammatory ways to label an issue and more opportunity for creativity and mutually beneficial solutions.

Second, once you believe you understand the issue and have framed it well, you need to *establish a goal* for the negotiation. Your goal may be to resolve a dispute between two students, to better understand the issues in a larger problem, or to develop a new policy. What is important is that you are clear about what you intend to specially accomplish. All too often we set our goals too broadly or fail to think about what we want to achieve in any given situation. When we state our intentions as "I want to solve the problem" or "I want this situation to go away" we set ourselves up for failure. Absent goals that explicitly detail what we intend, we lose our focus. Once lost, we bargain away resources we wished we had hung on to, or accept a compromise far short of what we hoped to obtain.

Car dealers are adept at capitalizing on our inability to clearly establish goals. People rarely walk into dealerships knowing how the cost of a car will translate into a monthly payment. This is why dealers work to move you off of the price of the car and into discussing the monthly payment. By focusing your attention on the check you'll write each month and not on the overall price, it is easier to sell you additional options or a more expensive vehicle. If you walk into the dealership with a clearly established vehicle price (including the options you really want) and know that at X interest rate you will pay Y monthly price on your loan, you are in a better bargaining position. You walk in having established your goal. By knowing what you want and asking for it you are more likely to get it (or something very close).

The third strategy necessary for successful negotiation and bargaining is to *identify what you have in common* with your adversary. Much like framing the issue, identifying common ground allows you to shift the issue to less confrontational ground. When we care about each other and solving the same problem we are more likely to find a solution that pleases everyone. Establishing common ground places the relationship rather than the problem first, and honors the people with whom you are working.

Furthermore, we spend most of our time negotiating and renegotiating with the same people. Because schools are places we come to day after day, adopting a "win at all costs" stance may secure you some early success, but in the long run it is likely to erode the trust of your colleagues. On the other hand, when we work to preserve our relationships as a primary goal of our problem-solving efforts, we invest in our common future.

One way to identify common ground as well as to understand the viewpoints of others is to *ask questions and listen to the responses*. Surprisingly, listening more and talking less can provide you with an edge in the negotiation process. This happens for several reasons. The most obvious is that people like talking about themselves and parents love talking about their children. As people talk about themselves, their problems and concerns, you have the opportunity to learn what they care about (making it easier to establish common ground) and to establish yourself as empathetic. Defensiveness is reduced and trust is established.

Empathetic listeners are perceived as caring and trustworthy. In turn, compromise is more likely as people are more willing to concede to people they view as having their best interests at heart. Problem solving is also easier because you have obtained more information and can use that information to the advantage of solution finding. Finally, questioning and listening keeps you from speaking too soon or saying something you might regret. It gives you time to think. Some ways to pose questions include:

- Uh-hum . . . .
- Say more . . . .
- That's interesting . . . .
- Why do you feel that way?
- Help me to understand . . . .
- How did you make that decision?
- And then what happened?
- What would you do in my situation?
- What would be a best-case scenario for resolving this?
- How did you arrive at that idea?

Once you have listened carefully to the answers to your questions, it is now time to begin working on crafting a solution to *the problem you share.* It is a commonplace of schools and other organizations that people like to drop issues on a superior's desk and walk away from the problem. The "you solve it strategy" is effective because it allows us to wash our hands of unpleasant business. However, if you are the kind of leader that accepts all problems big and small and jumps into solving them for others, you are probably a less effective leader than you might otherwise be.

Here's why. People support (and defend) decisions that they were part of making. It is easy to second-guess or criticize a solution that you were not part of designing. Because we tend to support that in which we have an investment, it is best to *gain the investment of the other party* in the problem-solving process. There are several ways to do this but the most effective is to move forward in the discussion using language that communicates your expectation that the other party serves an important role in finding a solution. In essence, you ask for help. Some ways to say this include:

- I'm looking forward to working on this with you . . . .
- Your ideas are interesting; let's get together to discuss them . . . .
- I like your thinking, let's call _____ into this discussion to help us hammer out the details.

- I'm not sure if I have all the data I need here. Can I count on you to get me _____ by Monday?
- I'm concerned that if we handle this issue the same way we always have, we won't solve the problem. What are some other options?
- Help me to think of a way everyone can benefit.

Asking for help flatters people. It telegraphs your confidence in them and creates mutual investment in the work that must be accomplished. Another added benefit is that after you've done this a few times, people come to your office expecting questions like these. They think about the answers before they even pose the problem to you and walk in already invested in helping you reach a solution.

It is important to note that gaining investment is not the same as delegating the problem to others. At times, careful delegation works. At other times, delegation moves you too far out of the problem-solving loop. When we are too far removed from framing the problem and establishing the goal, we are less likely to achieve a solution that benefits us. Just like you'd never let your neighbor negotiate the price you would pay for your new car, don't let folks who have less of a stake in the outcome negotiate important work-related issues either.

After gaining the involvement of others, it is necessary to *consider options and choices*. When we walk into a situation with a single rigid response we set ourselves up to lose. Identifying where you can be flexible in the negotiation goes a long way to solving the problem in a mutually acceptable way. Remember, part of your goal is to maintain your relationship with the people you work with day in and day out. Flexibility on some points allows you to say, "I'd compromise here if I could but I can't" more convincingly on others. If you have established yourself as someone who is reasonable, but just can't budge on this matter, you are more likely to reach a solution than if it's your way or the highway.

In this way, it is important to look at communication in problem solving as an ongoing effort. By working to establish good will across problem-solving issues, you can afford to be less flexible on occasion. Making concessions when you can, and providing acceptable options and choices, builds trust for future efforts.

In the end, problems must be addressed. We cannot spend all our time dickering over small details. Because our time is valuable, we must *set deadlines* for negotiation. Deadlines send two different messages about time. The first suggests urgency. The second allows for consideration.

When deadlines are tight and fixed, we are motivated to work quickly. When deadlines are loose or variable, we are able to spend more time thinking about a solution. As a leader, in most cases, setting the deadline is something you can control. Just as it is not necessary to accept a problem as someone else has framed it, you don't have to accept the deadline another sets either. When you control the deadline, you can control the pace and emotion of the discussion. If tempers are high, allowing a cooling-off period can give you much needed time to craft a more rational solution. If people seem to be dragging their feet on a matter, setting a tight deadline can motivate them to complete their work. Some ways to set deadlines include:

- Let me think about this overnight.
- I think we have some time to consider our options, let's meet on this again next week.
- This issue is important. Let's agree to have reached a conclusion by Friday.
- I will need to run this past the superintendent before we can move ahead with our plans. That will take two weeks; I'll need to have our decision by . . . .
- Are we pleased with our progress so far?
- How much more time do you think we might need to solve this issue?

Surprisingly, many people invest a good deal of time and effort in a negotiation only to leave the final decision unqualified. Think about times in your life when you thought you had reached a decision only to have the other party look at you and say that's not how they saw it at all. Closing the deal by *clearly articulating decisions and outcomes* seals the negotiation. At this juncture you can make the bargain. If they do this, you get that. If X happens, then Y will follow.

Depending on the matter, you may wish to informally write down the agreement, making a note of your expectations or you may wish to formalize the decision by drafting a new policy on the issue. In any case, each party

Table 4.3.   Successful Negotiation Strategies

Successful Negotiation Strategies
Understand the issue and how it is framed.
Establish a goal.
Identify what you have in common.
Ask questions and listen to the responses.
Gain the investment of the other party.
Consider options and choices.
Set deadlines.
Clearly articulate decisions and outcomes.

needs to be aware of and agree to the decision that was reached. The agreement serves to bind members to his or her role in the success of the decision as well as create a record of the process.

Done well, the negotiation process can strengthen the ties organizational members have to the school. As members communicate about what matters to them, we learn about their professional motivations and concerns. When we communicate well, our ability to move beyond superficial interactions is enhanced. As our interactions are deepened, our ability to complete meaningful work and lasting decisions is improved.

CONVEYING DIFFICULT MESSAGES

As leaders, not all of our communications allow for give and take. Sometimes we cannot negotiate. When our values and beliefs are questioned, when our purpose is under attack, it is necessary to communicate clearly and concisely why those things matter to us. Similarly, there are times when we must deliver bad news or relay a message that we are unhappy to share. In these cases, we cannot bargain another option and we must communicate with clarity and sincerity. We need to say (or write) what we mean and convey our thoughts with the conviction and empathy as the situation requires.

Communicating difficult news is an essential problem-solving skill for school leaders. Many of us feel unprepared or ill at ease in delivering unwelcome news. Whether it is news of budget cuts, the serious illness of a faculty member or student, or simply saying no to a request, the task is hard. Delivering difficult news well can make the difference in how it is received and how people respond.

When difficult news is framed well, the decisions that flow from it are more likely to be accepted. By framing difficult news thoughtfully we avoid creating new problems or making our existing problems worse. Here is an approach that works:

Before communicating difficult news, *develop a plan* for what will be discussed and how the discussion will proceed. Be sure you know all the facts of the issue and understand them. Define the issue clearly and simply. Decide who should be part of the conversation. This will depend on the issue. If the matter concerns student discipline it may be necessary to have a parent or teacher present. If the issue concerns faculty, it may be best to call a short meeting to share what you need to say. By including the right people in the meeting, rumors can be reduced and potential problems minimized.

If you are new to delivering difficult news or the situation is complex, you may wish to *rehearse what you will say*. Using notes is acceptable when the information to be shared is particularly difficult or detailed. In schools, there is not always adequate time to share news before the day begins. If your time is short, *prevent interruptions* and create an environment conducive to effective communication. Don't delegate the task. If the matter is important enough to call the meeting, it is important enough for you to be there.

Decide what your core message will be prior to beginning your conversation. Knowing your core message allows you to develop a mantra or broken record response that keeps your statements consistent and clear. It also allows you to reinforce the school's values and purpose as appropriate. Core messages might be phrased in these ways:

- In keeping with our commitment to shared problem solving, I must . . . .
- It is unfortunate that we disagree but I need to . . . .
- In order to best handle this situation I need . . . .
- School policy states that we . . . .
- We agreed that if _____ didn't happen we would . . . .

Deliver the information in a sensitive but straightforward manner. Rather than deliver a lecture or provide a long introduction, say what you need to say and then stop. It is certainly appropriate to thank people for coming to the meeting or to offer your regrets for disrupting their day but it is important to stay on point. It may be necessary to pause frequently and check for understanding if the issues are complex. It may also be necessary to stop for questions. Some ways to offer difficult news include:

- It's hard for me to say this . . . .
- Unfortunately, there's no question that . . . .
- I'm disappointed to share . . . .
- I regret that I must tell you . . . .

A word on using the phrase "I'm sorry." At times we are truly sorry and we should say it. Apologies are an effective form of communication when they are sincere. There are events that occur in schools that rightfully require our sympathy. However, we tend to use the words "I'm sorry" when we are simply looking for a way into a conversation. Furthermore, "I'm sorry" implies a personal connection to the event. By suggesting we are sorry we can inadvertently accept blame for what has occurred. When we are to blame we should own that, when we are not, introducing the possibility only muddles the issues. Often we aren't sorry but we *regret* the situation has turned out as it has. By saying, "It's regrettable," you can offer your sympathy for the situation and maintain your personal distance in the matter.

People respond to difficult news in a variety of ways. Some respond with tears or anger. Others react by expressing denial, blame, guilt, disbelief, or fear. Still others rationalize what is happening to them, suggesting that perhaps they might have avoided the outcome by making different choices. Outbursts of strong emotion make many of us uncomfortable. However, you can *be prepared for the response* difficult news produces. In extreme cases, it may be necessary to arrange for a social worker, police officer, or counselor to be present just outside the door. For less intense situations, quiet and attentive listening may be all that is required. If appropriate, acknowledge the emotions of the situation. You might say:

- Tell me about how you are feeling about what I just said . . . .
- I know this was important to you . . . .
- What worries you most?
- What does this news mean to you?
- Is there something you don't understand?

Establish a plan for next steps. This may include gathering additional information or offering to arrange for appropriate referrals. It may require that a small number of people get together to brainstorm how the larger community might deal with this event. This is your opportunity to have foresight. Since you are looking to avoid problems in the future from the impacts of this event, now is a good time to play the "what if" game:

What if these are only the first of the cuts?
What if we need to make drastic changes in the services we can offer?
What if students become unruly?

Of course, each "what if" statement requires that you proactively consider and problem solve our responses if the "what if" happens. By planning ahead potential problems are reduced.

Table 4.4.   Sharing Difficult Information

Sharing Difficult Information
Develop a plan.
Rehearse what you will say.
Allow an appropriate amount of time for the meeting.
Deliver the information in a sensitive but straightforward manner.
Be prepared for a response.
Plan for next steps.

At the root of all effective communication is the need to deliver a message that is unambiguous. Whether we are engaged in a negotiation or find ourselves in the position to deliver difficult news, some rules always apply:

- How we present what we say matters as much as what we say.
- Attention to the ways others see the world helps us to frame messages that get heard.
- Preparation provides us time to reflect on the situation, clarify our message, and consider our options and alternatives.

THE THREE C'S—CULTURE, CLIMATE, AND COMMUNICATION

A school's culture is characterized by deeply rooted traditions, values, and beliefs. Some traditions, values, and beliefs are common across schools. Some traditions, values, and beliefs are unique and embedded in a particular school's history and location. In either case, a school's culture informs the way "things get done around here." It is important to note that culture frames how communication is structured and received.

As a result of a school's cultural communication patterns, the school's problem-solving culture will differ. A very different problem-solving culture exists where communication is top-down than where it is more mutual and open. Top-down communication sets the stage for individual efforts. Mutual and open communication sets the stage for more collaborative approaches to problems. If you seek to intensify your problem-solving efforts and include others in the process, mutual and open communication patterns are needed for success.

Just as culture is defined as the way we do things around here, climate describes how we experience the places we work and learn. Upon entering a school building you experience a sense of how it feels to work and learn there. Some schools are warm and welcoming, others cold and sterile. Climate, too, is developed through communication patterns and efforts. As has been noted already, how we talk to each other matters as much as what we say.

In schools where the culture of communication is top-down but a trusting climate is present, teachers may be compliant and unquestioning. They may be used to receiving and following direction because they trust that the school leader has their best interests at heart. Problem solving may be less collaborative and creative; however, in day-to-day situations it may be effective because the leader's words can be trusted.

In schools where the cultural pattern of communication is top-down and trust is low, teachers may be resistant and defiant. If a leader's motivations are unclear or suspect, problem-solving solutions may be implemented or they may be purposely ignored. In this case, a leader might follow the identical patterns to solve problems as a more effective leader however; since confidence in the message is low, his or her results will be less consistent and powerful.

In this way, a school's culture and climate influences the ways communication about problem-solving efforts is received. Strong positive cultures and climates lend themselves to more effective problem solving. Weaker and more negative cultures and climates undermine problem-solving efforts and may contribute to the development of additional problems.

At this juncture you may be thinking that the solution to schools where the culture and climate undermine problem solving would be to change the culture of the school. Then, you might reason, the climate will be altered and problem solving would be easier and more effective. In theory, you would be correct. In practice, it's a bit more difficult.

Culture is difficult to change. Trust is easily undermined, communication networks can be fragile, and pockets of dissatisfaction can be divisive. Unexpressed assumptions of practice can undermine problem-solving efforts in unanticipated ways. On the other hand, a school's culture is the creation of its participants. For a culture to change, the participants must have a hand in creating the new structures that grow out of the old. Participation in and clear communication about problem-solving efforts can provide the foundation for culture-change initiatives.

In the end, how well school members hear messages about the school is, in part, based in how they experience working and learning in the school setting. When culture is unambiguous—members know what to expect and what is expected of them—culture is also strong. When culture is strong, communication is more clearly understood and problems are more easily solved. The process is recursive; problem-solving effectiveness benefits from the momentum built from solid and strong communication, which in turn makes communication efforts more powerful. As results accrue, the school's culture is strengthened and future efforts are more readily approached and addressed.

Communication can support or undermine problem solving in your school. The choice is yours. Ineffective communication creates barriers, generates additional problems, and weakens trust. Effective communication establishes foundations for creativity, teamwork, and cooperation. To make your communication effective, remember that *who* you include, *what* you talk about, and *how* you frame your message all contribute to success.

KEY POINTS

- Communicative meaning results when factual messages are received and understood within emotional contexts.
- How you interact with people matters as much (or more) than what you say.
- Negotiation is an ongoing process of involving others in problem solving to achieve mutual gain.
- Difficult messages require thoughtful presentation with careful attention to how the message is framed and what new problems may result.
- Strong communication about problem solving builds a strong school culture. In turn, a strong school culture can help make problem-solving efforts more effective.

CHAPTER REFLECTIONS

1. Are you a good communicator? Why or why not? How can you become better?
2. Are you a good negotiator? Why or why not? How can you become better?
3. Think of a recent communication. Answer the following questions about it:
   - How did the situation go?
   - Did I achieve what I needed?
   - Did the other person achieve what they hoped for?
   - What can I learn from the situation?
   - What could be done differently in a similar situation?
   - Where were the surprises?

CHAPTER ACTIVITIES

To communicate well we all need to understand how we think about our schools and the situations within them, how we label the issues that face us, and how we can talk with others about our concerns. Here are three activities that will help you do these things better.

Activity 1: Considering the Perspectives of Others

This short survey can help to identify some general areas of importance for a variety of groups in your school. If you choose to administer it widely, use different colored paper to keep your respondents separate. Comparing between group results can help you to understand how different groups see your school.

It is important to me that the school ...	Strongly Agree	Agree	Disagree	Stronly Disagree
Is a safe place				
Allows for individual expression				
Holds high expectations for students				
Offers interesting classes				
Is focused on learning				
Has clearly defined academic goals				
Operates as a team				
Provides for the professional growth of teachers				
Has a parent council				
Allows students a voice in the policies of the school				
Offers after-school programs				
Provides support services for students who are academically struggling				
Provides support services for students and families who are emotionally struggling				
Is a welcoming place				
Instills pride in each student for his or her efforts				

Activity 2: How Do You Approach Negotiation?

Good negotiation requires good communication. This quiz can tell you a bit about your negotiation style. Mark if you agree or disagree with each statement.

	Agree	Disagree
A quick response is best		
The best solution is a solution I create		
The problem that comes to me is the problem I solve		
Preserving the relationship is as important as solving the problem		
When a problem is solved everyone understands what is expected		
Making concessions can help obtain results		
It is possible to obtain a result that works and pleases everyone		
Involving others makes them more willing to support solutions		
Setting deadlines facilitates problem solving		
Providing options helps create solutions everyone can live with		
Asking for what I want makes me uncomfortable		
Part of the fun is the negotiation		
Asking questions provides useful information		
Finding common ground is often a first step to finding a solution		
You should be able to arrive at a decision within a single meeting		

- What did you learn about your negotiation style?
- If others, parents, teachers, or students, were to rank you on these same items, would they answer them in a similar fashion? In other words, are your responses backed up by your actions?

Activity 3: One Last Communication Quiz

Reflect on the communication tasks discussed in this chapter.

In the table below note your school's communication patterns.

Rank these as considerable attention (daily or at least weekly), some attention (monthly or quarterly), or minor attention (yearly or less). Also, note which areas are individual or team efforts.

Communication Task	Considerable Attention	Some Attention	Minor Attention	Individual	Team
Listening to teachers talk about what matters to them					
Listening to students talk about what matters to them					
Listening to parents talk about what matters to them					
Asking questions about the ideas others share					
Finding mutually agreeable solutions to pressing problems					
Identifying where your commonalities lie					
Framing differences as mutually understood problems					
Setting deadlines for problem-solving work					
Clearly articulating solutions as they are developed					
Sharing successes with others					
Planning for potential future problems or issues					
Gaining the investment of others in problem-solving efforts					
Focusing on mutual gain					
Culture and climate building					
Viewing problem solving as a communication effort					

Reflect:

- Where are primary communication focuses of your school?
- What areas are currently emphasized? Underemphasized?
- What areas are individual efforts? Communal?
- Where might more teamwork help the school attain its communication goals?
- How might the culture of communication in your school be enhanced?
- How might the climate of communication in your school be enhanced?

Chapter Five

Building Supportive Systems

When the only tool you own is a hammer, every problem begins to resemble a nail.

—Abraham Maslow

Effective leadership requires more than a hammer. Given the fact that school leaders deal with a variety of problems, it only follows that diverse solutions must be employed in addressing the issues we face. However, generating diverse solutions requires that leaders make use of multiple problem-solving tools, which in turn, must work systemically and together. This chapter will explore how schools function as systems, the importance of feedback and how to learn from feedback to enhance problem-solving efforts. The chapter will explore how school leaders can focus their energies on developing small, integrated systems that provide for enhanced organizational learning and build capacity for schoolwide improvement. In this way, organizational outcomes are improved through the use of strategies that support problem solving.

In this chapter you will learn why:

- Schools are complex systems.
- Systems are simultaneously predictable and surprising.
- Feedback systems are necessary to guide problem-solving work.
- Focusing on learning, for both the adults and students in the school, helps to build systems supportive of problem-solving efforts.
- School culture is a key determinate of systemic effectiveness.

What is a system? Very simply put, *a system is a set of things that, when integrated together, comprise a cohesive and coherent whole*. Together, the parts and pieces of a system function as one, creating complex structures and organizations.

Mechanical systems are comprised of gears, sensors, and motors that intermesh and power our world. Biological systems are made of tissue, bone, and muscle and support life. Social systems include people, families, and communities working together toward shared goals. In each instance, a system is created when the individual parts and pieces function as one, working together to produce expected (and unexpected) outcomes.

Ecosystems, for example, contain all the living and nonliving things within a natural area. The survival of the plants and animals within an ecosystem is reliant on the presence of food, water, heat, and light and each affects the biological processes within the system. Sunlight assists the growth of plants. Food and water ensure the well-being of animals. Plants take in carbon dioxide and produce oxygen. Animals do the reverse. When ecosystems are well integrated, plants and animals coexist, perfectly supporting and sustaining each other.

It might be easy to think that any group of things might be called a system. However, not all groups of things are systems. A bucket of water, a pile of rocks, or a group of people is not a system. Remove a single cup, one stone, or any member of the group and you still have a bucket of water, a pile of rocks, or a crowd. Ecosystems are systems because all the parts and pieces, the living and nonliving things, function as a whole.

Furthermore, not all systems operate smoothly. When one part or piece falters, the system can fall out of balance and fail. As we all know, a variety of factors can disrupt an ecosystem. When even small inputs change, the larger environmental outcome can be catastrophic. The success of the entire ecosystem may be at risk when even the smallest aspect of the system is disturbed.

As we can see from the example of the ecosystem, for systems to function well, the individual parts and pieces must function well. In this way, systems are more than the sum of their parts. Just as the health of an ecosystem is reliant on a variety of environmental factors, the overall behavior of any system depends on the entire structure. Like ecosystems, organizational structures rely on the smooth functioning of each operational area. Each organizational area must function soundly and be well integrated with the others, for the whole to be healthy.

SCHOOLS AS SYSTEMS

The comparisons of schools to ecosystems are clear. Like an ecosystem, a school's success is dependent on smooth functioning interrelationships between people, programs, and policies. When we invest time and energy in one part of the school we hope that those efforts will be rewarded and that the outcome of our work is positive. In turn, school leaders often hope that positive change in one area of the school or district will have a rippling effect and influence other less directly linked issues. Yet, when we change the system, even subtlety, we cannot always be prepared for the ways in which the larger system will respond.

If we think of the outcomes of our actions as events within the larger system, these relationships become more apparent. However, all too often we only see and respond to the events. We miss the broader scheme of things. We think we can break down a school into grades and departments or adults and children and deal with those parts as separate from the larger whole. We act as if the parts and pieces of our schools are interchangeable and do not affect each other. Common sense tells us otherwise. Some examples of these obvious interactions include:

- increases in student behavior infractions when schedules and practices are changed;
- changes in curriculum that, in turn, require in-service meetings that take away time from other pressing issues causing them to fester and worsen;
- potential negative outcomes for high-performing classrooms when an influx of inexperienced teachers joins the faculty.

Tinkering with any part of the school unavoidably affects other aspects of the school. This is why we need to think about *schools as complex systems*. If we think of the school as a system where numerous parts and pieces interact and affect each other we are better able to plan and prepare for potential problems.

Like ecosystems, schools operate best when we are able to integrate the efforts and energies of all members in achieving shared goals. Unless we attend to the way our policies and practices interact with each other and the people within the system, we are likely to find ourselves in a school with departments that may operate well autonomously but cannot integrate their efforts. Clearly, the presence of high-functioning teams, departments, and grade levels *within a school* contributes to the success of the school. However, when teams, departments, and grade levels function harmoniously *across the school* lasting progress toward goals can be achieved. Systems thinking can help school leaders solve problems because their attentions can be focused on the whole school rather than on smaller units.

EXAMINING YOUR SCHOOL'S SYSTEM

When considering problem solving within your school, analyzing organizational issues can provide you insight into the organizational big picture. Reflection on the big picture suggests that after problem-solving issues are identified, you consider the goals and outcomes you seek. It also suggests that by identifying the barriers to and facilitators of goal attainment within your school you can become a better problem solver. You might think of it as studying the system for the:

- issues that create problems,
- ways goals and outcomes are stated and discussed, or
- barriers to and facilitators of progress.

Considering Issues

When considering the issues that might affect the school, it is useful to consider issues that concern people and issues that concern structures. For example, *issues that relate to the people* within a school might include vested interests in programs or practices, relationships between and among staff, faculty, parents, administration, and other community members, and the levels of trust and respect that exist within the school. *Structurally centered issues* might include availability of resources including access to expertise to encourage organizational learning and time to focus on intended outcomes and goals, existing policies and regulations that may inhibit cultural change efforts, and the presence or absence of communication structures designed to foster conversation and dialogue.

Not surprisingly, for the school to efficiently and effectively function, how issues are addressed matters. People must be treated with respect and trust must be earned and developed. Resources must be identified and obtained. Poorly performing systems must be eliminated and new systems and structures must be developed in their place. However, knowledge of the complex factors and issues a school faces may not be enough to assure problem-solving success. Instead, the complexity of schools demands that we probe our understanding of issues more deeply.

Table 5.1. Types of Issues

People Centered	*Structurally Centered*
Vested interests	Available resources
Relationships	Costs
Traditions	Policies and regulations
Values	Communication structures
Trust and respect	Interdependence
Present and past practices	

Goals and Outcomes

It is best to start with considering how our goals and outcomes are communicated. For example, do you wish to "create inviting learning opportunities for students" or "raise test scores in reading?" Do you wish to "develop collaborative relationships among teachers" or "implement teaming?" "Increase trust between the school and surrounding community" or "increase parental involvement?"

As you can see, the first option in each of the choices above frames the outcome as an orientation to building school systems that support problem solving. The second choice frames the outcome as a program implementation. The first options strengthen school systems because they are more broadly stated and encourage the involvement of the full school community in the effort. By working toward the goal of creating learning opportunities, collaborative relationships, or trust, you can build systemic capacity for other efforts. By focusing on broad outcomes schools benefit in two ways. First, schoolwide problem solving becomes a central focus of activity within the school. As a result, school improvement activities are mutually understood and coordinated.

Barriers and Facilitators

Next, it is important to identify barriers to and facilitators of progress. Facilitators can include tangible resources such as time or access to grant funds and expertise. They may also include less concrete factors such as determination or resolve. Similarly, barriers can be concrete or attitudinal. When current systems do not allow for time to meet and plan, communal problem solving is harder. However, when leaders refuse to consider making changes to create time for much needed meetings, the barrier may be less about time and more about the leader's attitude. In either case, considering the barriers and facilitators to problem solving can head you in the right direction.

Table 5.2.   Barriers and Facilitators to Problem-Solving Efforts

Barriers	Facilitators
Unclear understandings of the issues facing the school	A clear description of the issue or problem to be faced
Inability to be objective about the issues that face the school	Determination to solve the problem
Intellectual defensiveness concerning change, new ideas, or ideas that come from the outside	Access to expertise
Inability to be creative with current resources	Interdependent leadership roles and mutually supportive responsibilities
Lack of internal or external resources	Time to meet and plan; grant funds; consultants to facilitate meetings

Once the barriers and facilitators have been identified it is useful to consider each. One might ask where supporting data exists to evaluate the validity of each, how significant a factor might be in implementing change, the relative strength or weakness of the factor, and where the most productive use of time might be invested. Here are a dozen questions to help guide your reflection and dialogue.

1. How important is each factor?
2. Does it support or hinder our efforts?
3. What data might we need to be certain this factor is as powerful as we think it is?
4. What information or skills might we need to make significant change related to this factor?
5. If we were to remove just one of the barriers, how quickly might we be able to affect change?
6. If we were to increase our support of one facilitating factor what additional resources might be required?
7. What areas seem to offer the most potential for success?
8. Which of these factors appears to be the hardest to address?
9. How are these issues related to our core purpose?
10. How might others view this issue?
11. If we change one of these factors, how might it affect the rest of the school? What might the consequences of change be for the school as a system?
12. Are there legal or ethical concerns involved with making this change?

The point of probing barriers and facilitators is to identify those aspects of the school system that help or hinder problem-solving efforts. The process allows school leaders to better understand the complexities present within the school. It also provides you the opportunity to examine the school considering the ways in which change enhances or disrupts the functioning of the whole systemic unit. Doing so helps to reinforce predictability and to minimize surprise.

PREDICTABILITY AND SURPRISE

When things are predictable, we can count on knowing what to expect in a given situation. Predictably allows us to plan for events in a routine fashion, presuming that the patterns we have come to expect each and every day will repeat themselves. Certainly there are times when the unpredictable occurs, but generally what happens in any school is much like the day before. In this way, schools are stable systems. Stability is important to knowing that day in and day out the performance of the school will be consistent.

This is, of course, purposeful. The success of the school as a complete system rests on the smooth functioning of the instructional program of the school. Structures exist so that schools can be organized in ways that minimize complexity. We want students and their parents, teachers, and support staff to be able to count on when school will begin and end, how the day will proceed, and the ways in which we will treat each other while we are at school. In an effort to keep people organized so that they may work toward instructional goals, we create structures so that life in schools is predictable. By creating structures within the school, we endeavor to manage the complexity of the school, increasing predictability and decreasing disruption to the system.

By developing uniform or standard ways of doing things we structure schools to be easily understood and negotiated. Structures that enhance predictability include:

- grade levels;
- teaching teams and departmental structures;
- courses, classes, and curriculums;
- semesters and quarters;
- passing time bells and other school schedules; and
- instructional methods and pedagogies.

Surprise!

However, when problems arise our predictable, ordered routines are challenged. When the unexpected occurs, we are surprised. Perhaps not surprised the way we are when fifty of our closest friends jump out and shout, "Happy Birthday!" but surprised by the failure of our systems to operate as we have counted on them to do so. Rarely, the surprise is due to a totally unexpected event within the school. While unexpected events such as floods and fires do occur, more often the surprise is the result of smaller and uncoordinated (or even conflicting) incremental changes.

If we think of predictability in complex organizations as being relative to the presence of logical, linear, and evolutionary change, we can see that numerous small changes can combine in unexpected ways, resulting in problems. Numerous small changes to school structures build layer upon layer, subtly altering the school's intricate balance. Eventually, older systems cannot bear the weight of the new changes and they tip, ever so slightly, and we wake up one morning and the school seems like a whole new place.

Since we can never know how the system will change, the challenge for leaders is not to try to plan for all the possible eventualities and surprises. Furthermore, doing so will not guarantee stability of the system because we cannot prepare for all possible outcomes. The trick, if there is one, is to maintain stability while remaining somewhat flexible and fluid. When we look at the systems in our schools as unavoidably and always changing, we are better able to adapt when we need to. Remember, we want the system to be stable so that things are predictable for the people who work and learn within it. Predictability helps get the job done. Surprises throw everyone off kilter.

To navigate between predictability and surprise, we need to learn how to adapt. In order to adapt we must be engaged in ongoing learning. Adaptation allows us to "learn our way" into systemic change, and be less surprised (or blindsided) when the system shifts. Adaptation is best nurtured in two ways. The first involves developing and paying attention to feedback systems within the school. The second entails creating smaller, tightly aligned systems designed to support learning from the feedback system and to generate new ways to face problems and challenges.

FEEDBACK SYSTEMS

Feedback can be thought of as *information about a system that provides one or more measures of how the system is performing.* Commonly, we think of feedback as positive or negative. Positive feedback tells us when we have done something well. Generally, we feel good about positive feedback. Negative feedback tells us we've done something incorrectly. Here the emotional response is less clear, some people feel badly, others get angry, and still others simply ignore the message.

As educators we've learned lots of ways to give feedback. Some of the most common include feedback that confirms, corrects, diagnoses, and explains or elaborates. For example, "Good job, you're right," confirms the correctness of an answer. Whereas, "You're close, think about adding punctuation," corrects a student's effort. Feedback can also diagnose, as when a teacher tells a student, "If you had done your homework, you'd be better prepared for class." Finally, teachers often use feedback as an opportunity to sneak in additional instruction, by elaborating or explaining an answer further, like when they say, "Correct, Mt. Everest is the tallest mountain in the world. Did you also know that it is located in Asia?"

Table 5.3. Types of Instructional Feedback

Feedback that...	*Provides information that...*	*Context*	*Such as...*
Confirms	Tells the learner if they are right or wrong	Generally used in positive feedback situations	You're right! Good job! Excellent! Well done!
Corrects	Tells the learner they are wrong and also offers the right answer or a hint about how to obtain the answer or fix the work	Generally used in negative feedback situations	Almost there, try adding the products together Delaware was one of the thirteen original colonies; however, Pennsylvania is where the Constitution was written
Diagnoses	Tells the learner where they may have gone wrong, made a mistake or how they might do better in new attempt	Generally used in negative feedback situations although it can be paired with positive feedback and used to motivate	If you would work more slowly, I'm sure you can find the correct answer to this problem
Explains or Elaborates	Tells the learner if they were right or wrong and offers more information on the topic	Generally used in positive feedback situations	Correct, Pi is approximately 3.14 and the symbol for it is π

The problem is that while educators are quite adept at *providing feedback* to students; we have, until only recently, had *limited access to feedback* about our own work. Certainly, we knew when parents were pleased or unhappy. We knew if the students in our class did well on the chapter test or not. We knew how far we had gotten in the math book this year as compared to last. We may have even experienced high-quality mentoring or coaching that provided us detailed feedback about our instructional or leadership style. But we knew very little about the relationship of our work to the achievement and progress of our students. Our assumption was that if students moved through the grades and subjects and performed reasonably well on the assessments we provided they would, in the end, have obtained an education that would prepare them for the world beyond the classroom. We assumed that if teachers taught and if students tried hard enough, they would learn.

Accountability changed all that. Accountability legislation suggested that schools needed to pay more attention to what students learned and how well they learned it. This irrevocably changed schools in two ways. Attention to what students were learning translated into the development of content area standards across the nation. Attention to the issue of how well students were learning gave rise to achievement testing.

Suddenly schools had lots of feedback. The problem was (and still is in many places) teachers, school leaders, and communities often could not make sense of what the feedback was telling them. Furthermore, even if they knew what the feedback meant they were often powerless to know what to do about the problems it presented.

Of course, the feedback to which I am referring is also known as data. Data comprise many of the puzzle pieces that leaders can utilize to build coherent school problem-solving efforts. Yet, prior to testing, schools were brimming with readily available data. So what is all the current fuss about?

Soft Data, Hard Data

What is new and is worthy of our attention are the ways in which we can collect data that measures our progress (or lack of progress) toward our goals. In the past, the data we collected could be described as anecdotal, descriptive, and intuitive. It was soft data. *Soft data* is personal data. Soft data suggests that our feelings in any situation provide us with important information about what is going on around us.

Because soft data is highly individual, it is often considered unreliable for major problem-solving efforts. If we are to spend thousands of dollars on a new text or program, we want to base the decision on more than a hunch or feeling. This is not to say that soft data is without value. Soft data can help us to understand, early in the problem-solving process, where things are (and are not) working and allow us to take corrective action. By paying attention to the feel of the building we can learn a lot about how our actions and efforts are being received. By talking to others about their sense of how a project is working we can learn a great deal about the potential effects of our decisions.

In the past decade, as a result of the accountability movement, much has been made about the introduction of *hard data* into the school problem-solving process. Again, schools have not been without hard data prior to the accountability movement. Grades, attendance and discipline records, enrollment trend, and graduation rates have all been sources of hard data for school leaders. The accountability movement and its partner, high-stakes testing, have introduced more and different forms of hard data into our schools. As was discussed in chapter 1, these data have both contributed to and helped to define our problems.

What both hard and soft data have in common are the ways they can contribute to the success of problem-solving efforts by providing us a way to evaluate our progress toward our goals. What they also have in common is the fact that they are readily available to us throughout the problem-solving cycle. We can simultaneously employ our existing data and actively seek out new data concerning the ways our decisions are making impacts into student learning and school experiences. In other words, hard and soft data compliment each other and provide us meaningful feedback about our results.

So how can we create schoolwide systems that are responsive to incorporating feedback and data into our daily problem-solving work? First, we must understand that *changing is not the same as producing results*.

- Change is about activities designed to reach goals.
- Results are about feedback concerning how well we have achieved what we are seeking.

CHANGE AND RESULTS

We claim change is hard. In fact, although change may require that we muster considerable resources and apply them to our problems, change itself is not that difficult. We do it often. In the face of new, compelling information, we readily change our beliefs and opinions. If you don't believe that statement, drop the term "presidential popularity ratings" into your favorite search engine.

Another example is technology. When offered new technologies we rush out to buy the latest cell phone, PDA, or MP3 player. In fact, even though popular use of the Internet is less than twenty years old, we are amazed when political candidates, our bosses, or parents (or grandparents) admit they can't or don't e-mail. In short, when we see a compelling reason to change we do so quite easily.

What is difficult is changing when someone else tells us we must. When we choose change, we have some *control* over the circumstances that govern our changes. Absent control over what must change, when it should change, or how the change happens we find it harder to transform our beliefs and actions. And so we resist. In problem-solving situations this complicates things because it introduces another variable into the system. Instead of being a simple process (setting a goal, locating a solution for a problem, and changing how things get done), the issues of control and resistance complicate the equation by introducing a mediating variable.

As mediating variables go, control and resistance are loud ones. In response to the growing cacophony of complaints, we get swept up in selling the change, procuring support, and making sure the change occurs. Exhaustion sets in and we forget what the change was supposed to accomplish, and instead, we count ourselves lucky to have managed its implementation in the first place. *By mistaking the change for the results it was intended to achieve, we shortchange whomever the change was meant to benefit.* By attending to the wrong feedback (getting through the change) we neglect an opportunity to obtain meaningful feedback about the system.

Poorly thought-out change initiatives can also produce poor results. Perhaps the district in this next case is a bit like yours. On a sunny August day, Thad MacGawain, principal of Whaller Schools' Comprehensive Secondary

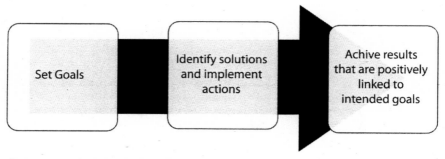

Figure 5.1.   Change as a simple process.

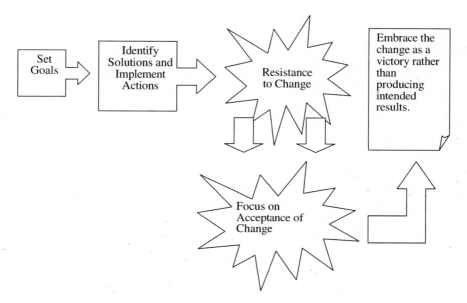

Figure 5.2. Resistance as a mediating variable to change.

School, welcomed faculty and support staff to a new school year. As he shared the school's goals and plans for the coming year, almost as an after-thought, he noted that the district was beginning a new data-warehousing project. Although he did not offer many details about the program, Mac-Gawain did say that he was excited to be part of this new initiative. It would, he hoped, allow us "to better understand what helped kids learn by collecting data on what they do and what we do with them." The teachers, anxious to begin readying their classrooms and organizing their first days and weeks, did not ask many questions about the initiative nor did they think it would affect them much. After all, as one teacher shared, "Every year it's something new."

After learning more about the warehousing initiative, MacGawain and the faculty were stunned by the amount of data the district office expected them to collect. Teachers had been requested to submit lesson plans, student work samples, chapter and unit tests, as well as records of classroom-discipline in-fractions and "any other records that have the potential to inform student learning decisions." The office staff was to keep track of student tardiness and attendance, parent calls and visits, and master a new discipline records man-agement system that tagged each infraction with one of twenty-five distinct and separate codes. MacGawain himself was required to keep a planner with his activities and to code them as instruction, personnel, community, or building related. He was also charged with managing the new computer-based report card project. The small conference room adjacent to MacGawain's office was soon overflowing with paper, printouts, files, and boxes.

At the urging of his faculty and staff, MacGawain asked district officials what they hoped to gain from the ever-growing collection of material. The curriculum director assured him that he was developing a plan to address how the district would warehouse the materials as soon as he finished analyzing the state-testing results. He went on to add that once the testing analysis was complete, the warehousing process would begin. However, he admitted that although he was "certain that this data collection would be fruitful," he was not "entirely sure" how the warehousing project would proceed.

Months dragged on. MacGawain, the faculty, and staff became less interested in collecting the materials and more disillusioned with the new initiative. Finally, in January, the curriculum director came to the school to share a presentation concerning Whaller's testing results from the previous year. Although the presentation was well conceived and presented, the faculty demonstrated little interest in the curriculum director's remarks. At the conclusion of the meeting, a teacher asked, "So what about all that stuff you wanted?"

The response? The curriculum director stated he'd have to "get back to them on that matter." MacGawain and the bewildered faculty sat silently.

The Whaller School District is a lot like other districts that have attempted data collection initiatives. Excited by the prospect of being able to collect data about student learning, they embark on well-meaning but overly complicated projects that, in the end, fail to deliver. These efforts often fall short because the people who initiate them fail to consider that data analysis, rather than data collection, is required if problem solving is to result. They mistake collecting a lot of data for the collection of *meaningful data*. Furthermore, as we become wrapped up in the process of developing systems to collect data it is easy to forget about developing the systems to provide for making sense from the data and, in turn, respond to the problem-solving needs of principals and teachers.

It is relatively easy to collect data. It is hard to determine what it might mean. It is even harder to determine how we can use what we learn to produce results. Collecting data is about looking like we are changing. Analyzing data and using the new knowledge we derive from our analysis to make decisions is change.

The difference is stark. In the first case, data collection is an end unto itself. In the second case, data collection is part of a larger system designed to enhance decision making with the intent of solving problems of practice. In the first case, we do nothing more than identify feedback from and within the larger system. No matter how hard we work, results cannot be achieved because the system was never designed to produce them. In the second case, all eyes are focused on creating new knowledge in an effort to examine feedback within and about the school. It is purposely focused on achieving results.

SMALL SYSTEMS WITHIN LARGE SYSTEMS

Focusing on feedback and results provides school leaders a clear path for creating systems focused on solving problems. However, results can be difficult to define. Results may mean increased student achievement, attendance, or parental involvement. Results may require curriculum changes, new data management structures, or school-discipline policies. Potentially, achieving results may mean that all these things need to occur. Producing all, or even a fraction, of these results requires that the school's systems function well.

By creating smaller systems within the larger system, leaders can assure that responsibility for the overall work product is distributed across the school. When responsibility is shared across smaller purposefully linked systemic units, the smooth operation of the larger system is ensured. Just like the human body where the digestive and circulatory systems support the well-being of the muscular and nervous systems, school leaders can create systems designed to promote the overall health of the school. In this way, a focus on results is more than a slogan; it is the glue that links our problem-solving initiatives together.

As members work toward commonly understood problem-solving goals they contribute to the larger system in distinct ways. It is important to note that the creation of smaller systems is more than distributing tasks to be completed. This orientation toward problem solving suggests that *there is deliberately broadened meaningful involvement.* It goes beyond saying that people will see their work as including problem-solving tasks. By deepening the *collective responsibility* for solving problems, accountability is expanded to include more people in the problem-solving system. Creating small systems goes beyond simply assigning work to more people; it demands that all members of the school community become active decision makers. Thinking systemically about problem solving suggests that participation in smaller complimentary efforts must be meaningfully and purposefully inhabited by faculty and staff across the school.

But what small systems are worth creating? How can we ensure that the work is meaningful and purposeful? Which smaller systems have the most potential to create high-quality results? Across the nation, several kinds of small systems have proven successful in urban, suburban, and rural schools. These include small systems that:

- promote individual and organizational learning,
- reinforce a strong school culture, and
- encourage the intensification of leadership.

Promoting Learning

Effective leaders seek to develop new and deeper understandings of how their school responds to pressure and change. While it may sound like a cliché, successful leaders see new challenges as learning opportunities. They seek to understand how one problem or decision might provide insight into other issues they face. Effective leaders learn from paying attention to the larger systems within the school and in concert with internal and external expertise, use their new knowledge to create and motivate change. Because it is collective rather than individual knowledge, this kind of knowledge is organizational in nature.

When we think of learning we tend to think about individual learning. Individual learning is comprised of the things each one of us knows and understands. Organizational learning differs in that it encompasses those things that are known and understood across the school. Organizational learning creates a shared knowledge base on which members may draw in the future.

Organizational learning (OL) is fostered when information is shared across the school and becomes embedded into the collective understanding and memory of the faculty and staff. However, OL requires more than collective in-service seat time. When a faculty engages in organizational learning they do more than individually absorb information that is provided to them. For OL to occur they must process the new information together and consider the applications of new ideas for their students, setting, and system. Leaders who foster OL provide ample opportunities for faculty to meet and talk together after new ideas and feedback have been introduced into the system.

Traditionally, schools have relied on the power of individual learning to carry school improvement efforts. Individual learning relies on sharing explicit knowledge. Explicit knowledge is a formal and tangible form of knowledge that is easily shared. Explicit knowledge is easily transmitted through memos, PowerPoint presentations, and lectures. It is static and often separate from the contexts in which it was generated.

Individual learning is important and necessary to promote best practices and current thinking. It is not, however, sufficient for growth. Nor is it nimble or adaptive in responding to rapidly changing environments. In environments where attention has been solely focused on the development of structures to support individual explicit knowledge, it is common for organizations to become stalled in the problem-solving process. Reliant on the good will and individual knowledge of each member, problem-solving efforts often fail because members lack sufficient understanding or support to implement new ideas.

In contrast, the development of organizational learning focuses effort on creating shared understandings and applications of knowledge throughout the school. OL consists of both technical and cognitive skills. It includes the know-how needed to get the job done and the experience-based skill set to know where the school currently stands and where it is headed. Additionally, OL is produced when together the faculty and staff interact within the school environment over increasingly longer periods of time and through distinctive experiences. It is fostered when teachers come together to process what they have learned and discuss feedback from the system that informs their understandings.

To encourage OL, school leaders must develop systems that are supportive of the creation and sharing of the knowledge within and across the organization. In turn, benefits are accrued schoolwide from collaborative attention to shared problems. Leaders who work to foster OL do so by creating opportunity for reflective meetings and discussions that:

- provide input regarding progress toward goals;
- examine puzzling or confusing data;
- foster thoughtful conversation about student achievement and progress;
- cultivate dialogue about formative and summative assessment;
- encourage the exchange of ideas about curriculum and instruction, teaching, and learning.

Finally, OL must become a regular focus of school activity. Just as it is not enough to provide in-service for individual learning, it is not enough to create small pockets of or intermittent attention to organizational learning. OL must be reinforced through the on-going efforts of school leaders. Leaders must regularly check in concerning what faculty and staff are thinking and discussing and employ those ideas in the problem-solving process for OL to make lasting contributions to change.

Reinforcing Strong School Cultures

A school that is engaged in OL is a very different place than a school that is not. OL cultures are marked by collaborative work, challenging dialogue and adaptation as new ideas are generated and tested. However, the transformation of a more ordinary school culture to that of a learning culture cannot occur overnight. Furthermore, it does not emerge as the result of a directive or command. Instead, it is created as deeply rooted traditions, values, and beliefs are replaced by newer, more useful behaviors, norms, and ideals.

A school's culture informs the ways in which "things get done around here" and, just as important, frames how problem-solving efforts are perceived. Although OL provides an avenue for changing the traditions, values, and beliefs of a school generally, culture is hard to change, even when the conditions appear right. This is because culture change relies not only on new ideas but it also relies on the ability of people to understand those ideas in the context of their school. To move from "where we are now" to "where we want to be" requires that we adapt our thinking. It requires that a new culture is created and that new culture is experienced as better than what went before. Culture only shifts when older ways of doing things are less attractive than newer ways.

However, shifting culture is more than simply making new ideas attractive. Shifting culture requires that we understand the norms that govern behaviors and the ways in which those norms shape our responses to our problems. As scholar Dan Ariely (2008) suggests, in any culture people are bound together by both social and market norms.

The best example of a social norm is the golden rule—treat others as you wish to be treated. Social norms bind organizational members to each other and govern the ways we treat each other and the ways we act when problems occur. Market norms, on the other hand, determine how much we are paid to do something, how much time we are required to put into a given project, and the value we place on our time and intellect.

Ariely argues that since social and market norms are distinctly different, how and when we employ them influences how well something will be accepted. For example, social norms are at play when we do a favor for someone else. If, in a school, one teacher asks another to cover her bus duty so that she might meet with a parent, social norms suggest that the bargain is accepted. Social norms also suggest that when after a few weeks the second teacher asks the first to cover his hall duty so that he might tutor a student, reciprocity is extended. Dependent on the school context, social norms might dictate that instead of reciprocity (an act for an act) a plate of homemade cookies might be proffered or a thank-you note sent. How social norms operate within a school contribute to the ways the school operates as a system.

For example, when social norms are at play we are willing to do something for someone we care about or respect, a cause we support, or an organization we are part of because it is the right thing to do. When the plate of cookies arrives the next morning, we find the thank-you note in our box or we offer to assist when someone who has helped us is now in need, our social connections are reinforced. In turn, it is strong social connections among teachers and staff as a system within the school that reinforces the school culture by strengthening the personal associations of members.

However, as Ariely notes we are less likely to give away things we believe we should be paid to do. Furthermore, we are more likely to do nothing when we believe our services are undervalued and underremunerated. Reconsider the scenario above. If the first teacher had approached the second and asked, "Will you take my bus duty for a plate of cookies?" a deal may or may not be struck. Once remuneration is introduced into the equation, the reward rather than the act becomes the focus. The second teacher starts thinking, "Is it worth it?" If the last time cookies were promised they were not delivered, if the teacher is on a diet, or he had just made cookies himself, the offer may not be sweet enough to entice him to give up the time after school.

Ariely's work demonstrates that as soon as market norms enter the picture, social norms fly out the window. Once we are asked to place a value on our work we are unwilling to do it for less than we think it is worth. From an economic standpoint, this makes complete sense. If our time, intellect, or skills can be sold, why should we give them away? Similarly, if the value of our work has been priced at one point accepting less than we believe we are worth makes us a sucker or a fool. Once a value has been placed on our work, market norms govern our reactions to the requests that come our way. In this way, our systems for doing things can be undermined by the introduction of market norms where they have not been present in the past.

So how can people be enticed to contribute to the overall good of the school? By creating strong cultures based on clearly defined social norms. This of course is the idea behind volunteerism. We are often willing to do things for free or for a small gift that we would not be willing to do if paid. Think, for example, all the friends you have helped move for pizza and beer. Had your friend offered you $9.95 for your Saturday you probably would be unwilling to sell your day. However, social norms suggest that friendship trumps the market.

From a culture standpoint, understanding a school's social and market norms helps school leaders nudge others toward new ways of doing things. Adaptations to the culture must be consistent with existing social and market norms. A leader is unlikely to be successful if he or she proposes changes that are well outside of current practice. On the other hand, we want to push the system just enough so that the system (and the people in it) adapt to new ways of doing things.

An exception to this statement would be a situation where the difference is clearly noted and a reason for violating the norm is presented. Contractual waivers allow for such events, as do special grants and programs. In these cases, the situation is clearly different and members may be able to shift more rapidly.

The point is that we want to identify social and market norms to foster learning within the school. By understanding "the way we do things around here," we are better able to develop new systems that are more likely to be accepted and embraced. Once we are clear about how our relationships are governed we can then use those norms to leverage systemic learning and systemwide improvement. Leaders who seek to develop culture change focus on creating:

- explicit ties between the old and the new,
- bridges between past practice and future work,
- compelling reasons for change,
- understanding about new ideas and practices and the ways they can benefit problem solving in the school.

In this way, adapting existing understandings to new ideas and ideals creates lasting culture change. The result is the development of systems within the school that bind faculty and staff to each other and the work of the school.

Encouraging Intensification of Leadership

Problem solving is a difficult task. Furthermore, it is an on-going challenge for any school leader. By including others in the problem-solving process, leadership can be intensified and problem-solving efforts enhanced. Intensified leadership opens the boundaries of leadership to include, in on-going ways, a wide variety of members of the school in new problem-solving roles. Furthermore, intensifying leadership requires others to become involved in generating new knowledge and ideas rather than simply carrying out existing organizational functions. In this way, intensified leadership acknowledges that expertise is present across the school organization and does not only reside in the principal's office.

Intensification presents several challenges for school leaders. The challenges include:

- identifying members' expertise,
- matching expertise with existing or potential problems,
- developing broad knowledge and skill sets (intensification is not about tapping only a small kitchen cabinet of internal advisors or consultants), and

- focusing the intellect and energy of faculty and staff on the core work of the school.

To identify members' expertise it may be necessary to do a short inventory of your faculty and staff. We often think we know the people we work with; however, explicitly inquiring about skills and talents of our colleagues often surfaces some surprising results. You may discover hidden musical, artistic, or literary talents, an interest in evaluation or assessment or perhaps a parent or community organization willing to partner on a tutoring or mentoring project. In any case you can't know where the talents of your internal and external communities lie unless you ask about them. You might start by listing the obvious needs of the building. Some areas you might want to look for expertise might include:

- collecting data,
- analyzing data,
- mentoring students,
- tutoring students,
- shared governance,
- classroom organization and management,
- cooperative learning,
- differentiated instruction,
- problem- or project-based learning,
- authentic projects and studies for student research,
- technology and learning.

Once you have completed an inventory it is important to start matching the skill and talents of your faculty and staff to the problems you currently face. The idea is to discover the ways in which you can capitalize on the resources that already exist in your school and community. In this way, as problems arise that require these skills the expertise is already identified and readily available. You already know whom to call on when a particular situation appears. Assigning small groups of teachers, staff, parents, or even students the responsibility for a manageable concern can begin the culture shift necessary to promote lasting change.

In some cases you may be aware that gaps of expertise are present or that the majority of expertise lies in the minds of a small group of veteran faculty. Intensifying leadership demands that all (or at least most) members of the school community are involved with some aspect of the problem-solving system. It may be necessary to deliberately work to develop the skills of less proficient or novice members.

Coaching or mentoring between and among faculty and staff has been proven to produce impressive results, as has participation in carefully selected professional development opportunities. No matter how a school leader goes about broadly developing the expertise of people in the school, it is important to do so on a regular basis. When opportunities for growth are provided, faculty are more willing to take risks and support improvement efforts if they know there is someone in the school supporting them. In this way, the overall school system is strengthened as are the individual skill sets of its members.

As the school develops small systems that encourage and support intensification, it is tempting for factions within the larger school to want to pursue their own agenda. To avoid this pitfall, school leaders need to be vigilant about linking the work of intensification, learning, and progress back to the core purpose and goals of the school and its students. On-going and regular check backs and communication systems can assure that as expertise develops and responsibility for problem solving intensifies, all members are moving in the same direction.

IN CONCLUSION . . .

Unavoidably our schools are systems of activity and effort. The issue is not that we are able to enumerate the number of systems that exist within the school or to go about creating systems where none are needed. Schools with lots of systems do not solve problems better than schools with few. Instead, effective problem solving rests on our ability to design and use systems that are supportive of the work we wish to accomplish. Furthermore, a school's systems are most supportive of problem-solving efforts when they are integrated and form a coherent whole. When systems operate coherently, the school hums along and the result is a smoothly functioning and effective learning environment.

KEY POINTS

- Systems thinking can help school leaders solve problems because their attentions can be focused on the whole school rather than on smaller units.
- Reinforcing predictability and minimizing surprise is the result of creating stable adaptive systems within the school.
- Data is feedback about how a school is performing in relation to its goals.
- Focusing on results rather than the activities designed to produce results is

the first step in creating schoolwide systems responsive to incorporating feedback and data into our daily problem-solving work.
• Creating smaller systems within the larger system can focus effort and reduce complexity.

CHAPTER REFLECTIONS

1. What metaphor would you use to describe your school? Is it like a machine? An amoeba? A family? Why does this metaphor fit and what does it say about your school?
2. How are your goals communicated? Do they address the unit as a whole or are they targeted on smaller units or tasks? How might they be strengthened?
3. What barriers to improvement exist in your school? What facilitators of improvement are present? How might the barriers be removed and the facilitators be reinforced?
4. How do you regularly use feedback in your problem-solving efforts? How might new feedback loops be built into the school's routines and procedures to facilitate problem solving?
5. What small systems are already present in your school? How can you capitalize on those systems to better link teaching and leadership efforts and produce student-learning results?

CHAPTER ACTIVITIES

You can explore how your school works like a system by completing these activities.

Activity 1: How Well Is Your School Linked?

In systems that operate well, all the parts of pieces of the organization are coherently linked. Try to link the variety of people, processes, and programs in your school.

• Start by making a fairly exhaustive list of all the projects in which you are currently involved.
• Write the name of each of the six most important projects in the circles below.
• Next list the people who are part of that work.

- Write the names of the people who are working on those projects in the diamonds near or around the project circle (you may need to add more diamonds).
- Draw solid lines that connect projects directly. Connect less tightly linked projects by dashes or broken lines. Do not connect projects or people that do not contribute to creating a coherent whole.

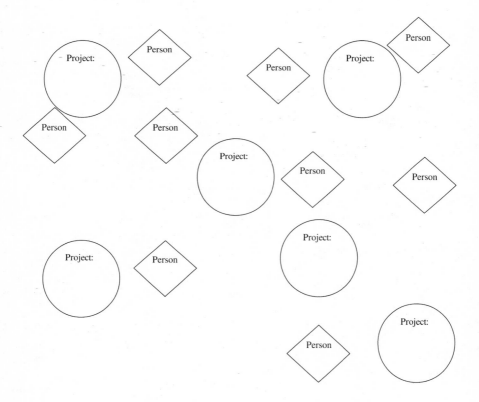

- What do you notice about how your school is linked together?
- Are there projects or people that are more central to the efforts? Less significant?
- How might you be able to link your leadership activities so that the work is more coherent and focused?
- What small systems are already present in your school?
- How might your existing efforts be enhanced to turn them into smaller more purposeful systems?

Activity 2: Considering the Ideal

In this exercise you'll use what you learned from activity 1 to develop an integrated, focused systems model for your school. To do so, consider the data you collected to complete activity 1, and use it to complete this school system diagram.

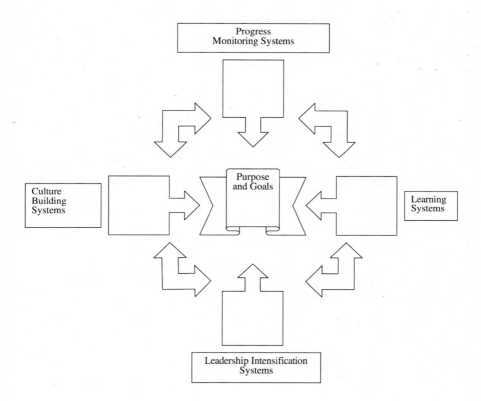

Activity 3: Leading Systems Change

This exercise is designed to allow you to take an organizational pulse. It helps to identify how systems are working (or not working) within your school. A single leader, a leadership team, or an entire school community may complete it. No matter how you choose to use it, this tool can help focus your efforts.

	Always	Most of the time	Rarely
Promoting individual and organizational learning			
1. All faculty and staff know and understand the goals and focus of school improvement efforts.	3	2	1
2. When new ideas are introduced into the school discussion focuses on issues beyond implementation.	3	2	1
3. Feedback from the system is used to determine how well the solution to a problem is working.	3	2	1
4. Individuals are encouraged to share what they know about the school with their colleagues.	3	2	1
5. Individuals are encouraged to share what they know about student learning with their colleagues.	3	2	1
Reinforcing strong school cultures			
6. Social norms are clear and explicit.	3	2	1
7. When change is attempted an effort is made to tie it to work that has gone before.	3	2	1
8. Faculty and staff feel that they share a purpose for their work.	3	2	1
9. Faculty and staff would identify the problems the school faces in similar ways.	3	2	1
10. Faculty and staff would identify the ways problems are being addressed in similar ways.	3	2	1
Monitoring progress toward goals			
11. Data is collected in an on-going and meaningful way to inform problem-solving efforts.	3	2	1
12. Progress toward goals is identified and celebrated.	3	2	1
13. Clear targets for performance and growth are set and understood by all faculty and staff.	3	2	1
14. Data are analyzed and discussed in productive, professional ways. The attention is on improvement rather than assigning blame.	3	2	1
15. A variety of data are collected and multiple viewpoints concerning its use in problem-solving efforts are encouraged.	3	2	1
Encouraging the intensification of leadership			
16. Problem solving is a group effort.	3	2	1
17. Faculty and staff know where expertise is located within the school and can call on others' knowledge to assist in problem-solving efforts.	3	2	1
18. When problems are present, effort is made to determine which systems might best be used to address the concern.	3	2	1
19. It is commonplace to see groups of teachers working with each other on common concerns and problems.	3	2	1
20. A variety of members of the school are engaged in problem-solving efforts.	3	2	1

Chapter Six

Constructive Policy

The measure of success is not whether you have a tough problem to deal
with, but whether it is the same problem you had last year.

—John Foster Dulles

In the last two chapters we have seen how effective communication and supportive systems can positively influence problem-solving efforts. A third important support for problem solving includes the policies that are part of the
school's operational and improvement strategies. Policy sets the school on a
course of action. When school leaders construct policy they create expectations for how students and teachers will act, how instruction and curriculum
will be put into practice, and how the school will respond in times of crisis
and stress. This chapter will provide a roadmap for creating policies that enhance and support problem-solving efforts.

In this chapter you will learn why:

- Sound policy development is essential to successful problem solving.
- Linear models of policy development are not robust enough to guide
  leaders in problem-solving efforts.
- Attention to multiple streams of policy activity and designing networks to diffuse the work of problem solving across the school and
  the community can enhance success.
- Seeking support and critique in the policy-development process is
  important.
- Successful problem solving is influenced by a leader's perspective.

To understand how policy can influence problem-solving efforts it is useful to begin by understanding what policy is and how policy is developed, implemented, and evaluated. In simple terms, *policy consists of the formal processes and procedures created or adopted by an organization that assure consistent responses to similar situations*. Policy is written because developing guidelines and procedures to make certain that similar situations are handled in comparable ways can help to solve existing problems and to avoid the creation of others.

Of course, everything that happens in schools is not informed by written, clear guidelines. All schools have unwritten policies concerning "how we do things around here"; however, they are more a part of the school's culture than of its operational processes and procedures. Policy does not usually address the informal aspects of the school. Reserved for the formal procedures and practices and expected of all members, policy is designed to assure the smooth functioning of the school. Most schools have one or more policies that address:

- the behavior of students, faculty, and staff;
- how emergencies should be managed;
- technology use across the school and district;
- instructional, curricular, and assessment programs;
- issues of wellness, nutrition, safety, and security within the school;
- maintenance of property and equipment;
- boundaries of and for attendance, enrollment, transportation, and participation;
- purchasing materials and awarding contracts and agreements for service.

The list is virtually endless and is always subject to revisions and additions. In this way, policy development and use is not a stagnant process. Instead, it is active and evolving, responsive to the changes within a school's environment and context.

When clear and focused policies are constructed, problem solving is enhanced. Policy helps school leaders to identify problems, initiate actions, and evaluate results by assuring fidelity and reliability throughout the school. *Fidelity* means that people behave in expected ways. Policies focused on fidelity assure that the activities that a leader intends to happen do, in fact, take place. For example, a policy focused on fidelity would monitor that teachers implement a new curriculum as adopted.

Reliability means that people behave in consistent ways. Policies focused on reliability make certain that what someone does on Monday resembles what they do on Tuesday. For example, leaders would expect that student codes of conduct be implemented in reliable ways, assuring that students are treated equally when similar violations occur.

Assuring fidelity and reliability is a primary responsibility for school leaders. An integral part of the policy evaluation system includes attention to the ways in which new policies and practices are (or are not) incorporated into the work of faculty and staff. It makes little sense to go to the trouble of creating new policy only to have it be ineffectively implemented and utilized. Furthermore, the inconsistent application of policy can lead to increased problems if, for example, some groups of students, faculty, or parents feel they are singled out and treated inequitably. Without fidelity and reliability, the problem-solving effort can be undermined. When this occurs, not only is organizational trust diminished, but also the efficacy of the school leader may be eroded.

POLICY DEVELOPMENT

The process of developing and implementing policy involves attention to a variety of elements that interact over time. These elements include:

- Stakeholders—including parents, faculty and staff, students, community members, district leaders, and state and federal officials.
- Time—potentially spanning months or years, including the emergence and identification of a problem requiring that policy be developed or revised, data collection and analysis, implementation, and, ultimately, the evaluation of impact.
- Competing programs or policies concerning the matter—including district, state, or federal mandates and legislation that unavoidably influence the scope of work required or allowed.
- Debate and disagreement—including disputes about the causes of a problem, its severity and importance, potential solutions and their costs, as well as the impacts of alternative policy solutions and choices.

Consideration of these elements leads us to the conclusion that policy is:

- influenced by a wide variety of people with
- differing understandings of the issues at hand, each with an
- interest in the outcome, that occurs
- over time, and can be
- influenced by ideas and anxieties far beyond the schoolhouse door.

No wonder why policy development and implementation can be so difficult.

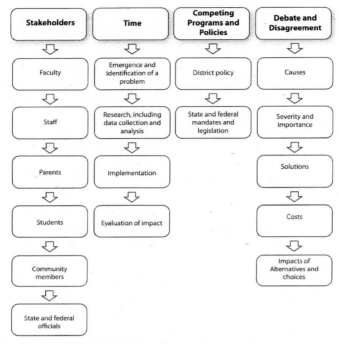

Figure 6.1.   Elements that interact and affect policy development.

LINEAR POLICY MODELS

Yet, policy is necessary for schools to function well. It is important that members know what is expected of them and how they are to respond in a given situation. When thought of in this way, policy development appears to be a straightforward and linear process. The process might look a lot like this:

- recognize a problem exists;
- document when and how it occurs;
- gather input and ideas concerning a policy solution that requires school-wide compliance;
- design policy to ensure the solution.

The linear process of policy development suggests that from the earliest stages of recognition through implementing outcomes, each step can be contained and completed in a discrete fashion. However, critiques of the linear model suggest that it is descriptively inaccurate. Any experienced school leader knows that policy development rarely follows such a clean and direct

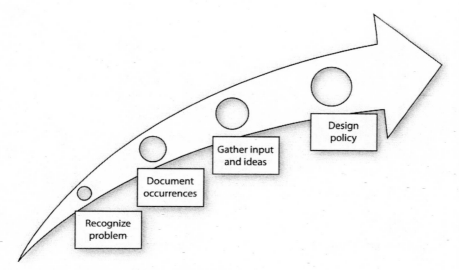

Figure 6.2. Policy development as a linear process.

path. For example, during the implementation of a new policy new, but related, problems might arise. In this way, stages may overlap and intersect rather than proceed in a linear manner.

Furthermore, the model assumes that issues requiring policy solutions appear one at a time in an orderly fashion. The linear model does not account for the variety of issues that arise on a daily or weekly basis, nor does it explain how leaders might manage the interaction of several coexisting problems. It assumes that a leader's time and energy can be focused on one all-consuming important policy issue. Here again, experienced school leaders know that often multiple issues are present within the school requiring attention to policy. For example, the dress code may need to be revised and at the same time a new policy regarding cell phones, I-pods, or Sidekicks might be needed.

Finally, the linear model assumes that in any given situation a school leader controls the policy-development environment. The linear model fails to consider that the actions of others may well affect the work product at any single school. New state legislation can affect the ways in which school leaders are required to address policy they had previously considered complete. Likewise, some issues, such as health curricula, are subject to ongoing critique. For example, opponents of sex education can be simultaneously involved in litigation, program evaluation, and critique as well as trying to affect the ways teenage sexuality is conceptualized. In such a situation, the variables are neither linear nor controllable.

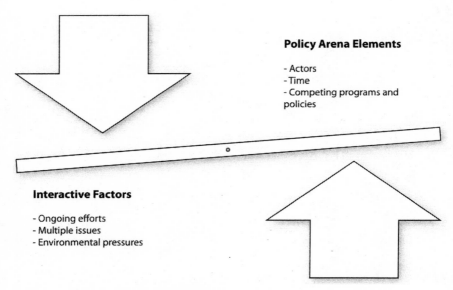

Figure 6.3.   Tensions with the policy-development process.

In this way, ever-present elements (such as stakeholders, time, competing programs, and disagreement) within the policy environment affect the ways in which policy development can proceed. These elements, in concert with other interactive factors, diminish the utility of the linear model.

NONLINEAR POLICY-DEVELOPMENT MODELS

If linear models are not robust enough to provide direction for the development of constructive problem-solving policies, what models offer more guidance? Like problem solving, policy development is best described as a mutually informing, iterative cycle of activity and feedback. Consider the way policy development happens at Atwood-Field High School.

Atwood-Field High School policy-development efforts have two distinct facets. First, there are the policies designed to inform students and faculty about the rules and traditions that directly affect them. A student handbook addresses issues of attendance, dress, behavior, and discipline codes, cell phone policies, calendar, scheduling and credit hour requirements, bullying and hazing policies, and the like. There is also a faculty handbook. The handbook is comprised of district polices not outlined in the collective bargaining agreement. Included in it are policies regarding study halls and fire drills, field trips and summer school, open houses and homework, testing, supplemental book selection, and other matters that affect teachers' work.

Second, there are policy or practices unique to the school. An outgrowth of the school's now defunct site-based leadership team, the guidelines present in the policy-practice agreement are written down. However, unlike the policy manuals that outline legally or contractually required directives, the policy-practices guide includes the agreements faculty and staff have made with other members of the school community to address issues of importance. To an unknowing reader it looks like a set of bylaws, in which a committee structure for the school is outlined and membership and charges for each committee are described. However, in use, the guide serves to set out an ambitious agenda for policy development in the Atwood-Field school community.

The guide charges three multidisciplinary committees with tasks related to curriculum review, instructional improvement, and assessment practices. It charges three additional committees with the tasks of mentoring and coaching new faculty, developing and offering student tutoring and support services, and community involvement and outreach. As described by a French teacher, "The policy teams exist so that we are all involved with running the school. We all have input into how decisions are made and how things get done. Everyone has a role; you have to be on at least one committee. You can't escape it."

He adds, "The old site-based team was good and all, but it didn't really work all that well to deal with the kinds of things that we thought needed to be talked about. There was too much to do for them anyway. With policy/practices, each committee chooses an issue to work on each year and we get it done."

Communication about the work of the committees is enhanced by an executive council. The chair of each committee attends a monthly council meeting so that efforts are coordinated and communication is open and direct. Discussion about each committee's tasks and activities is also a part of departmental meetings, staff in-service days, and formal full faculty teacher meetings. In this way, activities across the school can be interwoven with departmental and faculty work. While communication isn't always perfect, this format does create more channels for faculty and staff to be aware of what is happening across the school.

Most important, as both a policy and a practice, the committee structure works. It ensures that each year at least six key issues are considered and addressed. Current policy and practice is regularly scrutinized for how it can be improved and changes evolve from faculty examination and review. The committees guarantee broad input from faculty and staff across the school and include a system for parent and student input as needed. Moreover, it is transparent. When the work of a committee does result in new or revised policy, the faculty and staff have been aware of the work in progress and have been able to provide input into the final product.

As an art teacher notes, "Before policy/practice we looked like we had input into what happened in the school, but we really weren't all that hands-on. Now we work together on our stuff. It ain't always pretty—we often disagree before we agree—but in the end we're better for it."

What makes the policy context at Atwood-Field unique is that it is characterized by multiple streams of policy activity enhanced by strong networks of support. The policy-practice model works because it simultaneously attends to several layers of policy development and fosters an environment where all stakeholders have a role and where debate and disagreement are encouraged as part of the policy-development process. Ultimately, the process is successful because it focuses on three streams of activity:

- A *collection phase* where the elements of the school environment are thoroughly researched and problems become known.
- A *selection phase* where, after debate and disagreements have surfaced, mutually favorable solutions are developed and formalized.
- A *reflection phase* where implementation and evaluation concerns are openly addressed and successes celebrated.

Table 6.1 illustrates how each of these streams of activity interacts with the elements of the school policy arena.

Furthermore, the model works because it utilizes the data collected and the energies of faculty and staff, community and students to produce results. Effort is diffused across the system and networks of support are developed that ensure communication and collaboration. The process also immunizes the school against missing potential issues or ignoring simmering problems. A single leader—or even a small team of dedicated staff—cannot look for, and see, everything.

As we have explored already, how individuals view the school, and the policy needs within it, is governed by their own unique sensitivities to the school environment. Thus, different school leaders can look at the same situation and see things quite differently. The policy-practice model builds into its process attention to multiple streams of activity within the school and the different lenses with which those activities might be viewed. Finally, since the process is transparent it remains open to a variety of explanations of and solutions for the problems that a school faces. In this way success is enhanced as the policy that is ultimately created has been widely debated and accepted prior to its adoption, and evaluation is built into the system.

Table 6.1. Multiple Streams of Policy Development

		Interacting Elements of the Policy Arena		
	Stakeholders	Time	Competing programs and policies	Debate and disagreement
Collection	A variety of potential issues and concerns are researched and vetted.	Timelines and outcome goals are set and widely understood.	The policy environment is recognized and acknowledged. Barriers and facilitators to progress are identified.	Potential areas of disagreement are identified and surfaced. Obstacles are acknowledged and channels of agreement developed.
Selection	Through the use of mutually agreeable criteria, favorable solutions are identified.	Attention to timely and appropriate action is the focus of school leaders' work.	Given the current environment, favorable solutions are identified.	Critical and constructive dialogue is encouraged as members work to create lasting and durable solutions.
Reflection	Implementation and evaluation processes are created and examined for efficacy.	Forward-thinking leaders work to anticipate how policy can evolve to support further growth.	Progress is measured, unanticipated problems are identified, and successes are celebrated.	Prior concerns are revisited with attention to stakeholder satisfaction with policy outcomes.

Multiple Streams of Policy Activity

The policy-practice model creates a structure in which constructive policy development and problem solving can occur. In less functional policy environments, information is often collected but not used in decision making, or task forces expend considerable time on a project only to be told, at its conclusion, of barriers that exist impeding its implementation. In these cases, trust is eroded and engagement in school policy work is discouraged. The "all eyes open" approach to policy development enhances meaningful engagement in issues of importance to the school and ensures that the process of developing policy increases purposeful connections between and among faculty and staff.

SEEKING CRITIQUE AND SUPPORT

Ultimately, school leaders are the individuals responsible for policy-development efforts within the school organization. However, the success of policy development and implementation efforts is reliant upon the goodwill and support of all the people that comprise the membership of the school. In this way, involving others in the policy-development process is only smart.

Even if you are a leader in a building where a process as comprehensive as that of Atwood-Field is not possible, smart leaders find ways to incorporate the talents of teachers, parents, students, and community members into the policy-development effort. Teachers and others can provide the school community rich sources of imagination and creative energy. In turn, school leaders can rely on their wisdom and insight in the policy-development process.

Some leaders identify a kitchen cabinet of trusted advisors. Dependable and reliable, a kitchen cabinet can help leaders navigate rough waters. An obvious way to create a kitchen cabinet of your own would be to identify key leaders throughout the school and community and call a monthly meeting to listen to their sense of how things are going. The group could be formalized into a leadership team, a task force on emerging issues, or a committee on school success. Membership could then evolve fluidly, with attendance determined by the issue at hand or remain more restricted, as long as attention is paid to sharing the discussion so that others can be privy to what was talked about.

In any case, effective leaders incorporate the assistance of others creatively. Beyond including others in brainstorming, some leaders identify people to act as muses, critics, or pragmatists. In these examples, their input is used less to hammer out the details of a policy and more to inspire new thinking and creative solutions.

Muses provide leaders with someone whose input they seek when they want to dream. Dating back to Ancient Greece, muses were godlike creatures who served to inspire authors, composers, and leaders to do their best. In modern times and practical terms, a muse can be a trusted friend or confidant, a consultant, or a mentor. A muse is someone with whom you can bounce ideas around and try out unlikely and far-fetched thoughts. A muse serves to encourage creative responses to ordinary problems. They know the organization well enough so that their feedback is helpful but are distant enough to stimulate new thinking.

Critics, on the other hand, provide someone to point out the potential pitfalls of an idea. The best critics are able to offer constructive feedback concerning the ways in which an idea might be refined or improved. When leaders need to know the variety of ways any idea can go wrong, the critic is your best friend and mentor. Leaders who have ready access to a thoughtful and perceptive critic can forestall policy failure.

Pragmatists aid leaders to bring lofty ideas in for a landing. They serve to help inspire intelligent thinking while cautioning against folly. Unlike the critic whose job is to find error, the pragmatist seeks to find the elegant solution. They seek to uncover the most straightforward policy solutions. In this way, pragmatists help leaders avoid misfortune and create environments where opportunity can flourish.

Whether it is the services of a muse, a critic, or a pragmatist, effective leaders think about the kinds of support they need to become the best leader they might. In this way, they assure themselves:

- access to internal and external expertise,
- time to reflect and respond, and
- personal distance from the problems at hand.

Access to internal expertise matters because, when power and authority are shared across the school, thinking about problems in diverse ways is encouraged. As internal expertise is developed and encouraged, individuals within the school are better able to serve in mentoring or coaching roles, provide expertise in data collection, and analysis in the arena of governance. The overall effect is that not everyone is engaged in every aspect of an improvement agenda but all are engaged in contributing toward shared success.

Access to external expertise matters because at times the answers cannot be found within the walls of even the most capable school faculty and staff. At times, fresh eyes are required to see why a situation has not been resolved or to offer suggestions concerning how a policy might be improved. By regularly including others (such as parents, community and business leaders, and the personnel that nearby colleges and universities can offer) in the school policy-development efforts, external expertise becomes more easily accessible. Without continued opportunity for growth in the knowledge and skill set of the school, it is unlikely that sustained growth can be supported. External expertise can assist in providing robust solutions to the complex problems schools face.

Creating *time to reflect and respond* helps leaders to make good policy choices. Reflection creates the space necessary for learning to occur in the policy-development process. When we have taken the time necessary to better understand the situations we face, we can, in turn, be more informed and creative about the ways in which we can more effectively solve them. Conversely, impulsive actions create poor policy choices. When we act without considering the variables at play or without making an effort to consider the potential impacts of our decisions, our ability to reasonably defend our choices is diminished.

Personal distance from the problems at hand allows us to separate ourselves from the situation. Good leaders understand that the work they do is ultimately not about them. Instead it is about creating a school environment that fosters the best conditions for adult and student learning, progress, and achievement. All too often, leaders get swept up in making choices that serve to enhance their reputation or are reliant on personal charisma and appeal to get work done. While this might be effective in the short run, in the long run such solutions rarely make for good policy as the motivation of others to comply is removed when a leader leaves the school or moves on to a new project.

Developing personal distance from the situation can help leaders to be more objective about potential causes of and solutions for issues as they arise. In this way, more effective policy can be developed and implemented. In turn, examinations and evaluations of results can be more impartial as policy is less someone's pet project and more about schoolwide success.

At the end of the day, the school leader's role in policy development is to create a supportive environment where multiple streams of policy work can occur in tandem, resulting in the development of lasting policy that enhances a school's core purpose and goals. By creating supportive environments for policy-development work, leaders can create better policy. Better policy leads to better, more functional schools.

WICKED PROBLEMS

No matter how hard leaders try there are some problems that defy policy solutions. In fact, they seem to defy any solution at all. Known as wicked problems, these issues have vague, incomplete, contradictory, and changing requirements. Wicked problems arise when a school is forced to address something new, when change is required, or when multiple stakeholders have different ideas about how a decision should happen.

The hallmark of a wicked problem is divergence. If the issues a policy is to address keep changing, if stakeholders can't agree, or the requirements for a successful solution keep changing, you are most likely dealing with a wicked problem. In schools, wicked problems cover a variety of issues as widely reaching as:

• resource attainment and allocation,
• school reform and improvement,
• testing and assessment,
• community involvement and engagement, and
• student rights and responsibilities.

Wicked problems arise again and again, challenging the most capable school leaders. While some problems, like student achievement and success, are simply enduring, others are exacerbated by several contributing conditions. These include a lack of trust, scarcity of resources, and environmental turbulence.

An absence of *trust* can have negative consequences for a school leader. When faculty, staff, and parents do not believe they can trust the principal or superintendent, this barrier may undermine the policy-development process. Schools require cohesive and collaborative relationships to establish lasting and durable policy. Leaders that act in predictable, reliable, and competent ways enhance trust. Predictable leaders act in ways that teachers and parents learn to rely upon and to depend. Predictability allows teachers and other school community members to trust that a leader will use and enforce the policies of the school. Similarly, reliable leaders act in a dependable fashion fostering respect for their leadership skills and abilities. As leaders act in predictable and reliable ways, teachers and staff see them as competent to do the job well and, in turn, increased trust grows. When a leader faces wicked policy problems, trust becomes an invaluable resourse to draw on.

Other resources that are required when dealing with wicked problems are time, money, and expertise. *Scarcity of resources* means not having the sufficient resources to attain the goals a school has set. Scarcity implies that not all of a school's goals can be attained at the same time, so that we must trade off one potential good against others. When resources are scarce, we tend to focus on small short-term issues at the expense of losing touch with our long-term goals and objectives. Discussions can become stuck as we focus on what can be done next week, on a shoe-string budget, rather than considering what might be best in the long run.

Since this is the case, issues of scarcity must be addressed at the start of any wicked policy problem and treated as part of the problem rather than as a barrier to a solution. This is not to say that school leaders should ignore issues of scarcity. Clearly, attaining resources for the school is an important aspect of any school leader's job. However, waiting for a better day is often not possible and policy must be developed in light of the resources we have rather than those we'd like.

It is well documented that schools today are different from schools of past decades. If we accept that today's schools are different, we must also embrace the notion that change is inevitable. Part of any change is *environmental turbulence*. Environmental turbulence may be produced from any number of places. Turbulence can be the result of internal or external conflict. It can also be the result of complexity in the social or political environment surrounding the school. Even the best school leaders cannot control environmental turbulence. However, they can prepare for turbulence using strategies and approaches that are as flexible as possible. Even in wicked policy situations savvy leaders understand that being willing to change course or to reconsider a prior decision can help to alleviate environmental tensions. In this way, although the problem may not be resolved, as the leader you'll still be there to fight the good fight another day.

When addressing wicked problems it is best to keep in mind that the enduring dilemmas of school leadership—student achievement and progress, community and parent involvement, safety and security, resource attainment and allocation—are present in all schools and school districts and are reoccurring. Realizing that at best, an effective school leader can arrive at a sufficient but temporary solution, school leaders must be prepared for the next round of issues before they arise. Preparation includes attention to developing policies and practices that create readiness in faculty and staff to continue to address new problems as they develop.

SUCCESSFUL PROBLEM-SOLVING LEADERSHIP

The chapters of this book have each taken on a separate aspect of the problem-solving context. We have seen how purpose contributes to effective problem solving and how attending to identifying problems, initiating actions, and evaluating results can provide school leaders a way to make problem solving an active part of their leadership practice. We have also discussed how effective communication, supportive systems, and constructive policies can all contribute to more successful problem-solving practice.

While this serves an instructive purpose, in conclusion it is worthwhile to include some discussion designed to tie the separate pieces of the problem-solving model and the ideas discussed in this volume together. To that end, let's take a moment and consider how school leaders talk about their problem-solving work.

When talking about problem solving, school leaders employ any number of metaphors when describing their work. Like Sisyphus, some see themselves as engaged in the act of eternally pushing a boulder uphill only to watch it tumble down. Others describe their work as a rollercoaster of challenging ups and downs. Yet, in the end they find themselves further along than when they started. Whether you see yourself as endlessly and futility addressing the same issues or as facing new challenges daily is based on how you choose to see your work.

Your perspective matters. We can choose to see the problems that we face as never changing and immutable or we can see them as possibilities. Problem solving, like life, provides us opportunities, possibilities, and choices. Our ability to experience our circumstances as transformable and transformative depends upon our ability to see our schools and ourselves as able to change.

Problem solving is both simple and hard. It is simple because we can choose to employ strategies and practices that enhance our ability to be successful. It is hard because schools are places of enduring dilemmas. The difference between leaders who view their work as Sisyphean and those that do not is perspective. Sisyphean leaders believe that in the end their work will have no impact or importance. Leaders who grasp onto possibility and hold tight, realize that the sum of their efforts adds up to far more than even they might have intended. The difference lies in their perception.

What follows are the puzzle pieces that contribute to embracing problem solving as possibility. Each appears within the text in one form or another. However, they are worth repeating once more. They are derived from one of the key themes of effective problem solving—*by focusing on what matters you are more likely to succeed.* Quite reasonably, effective leaders spend their time and attention on significant issues and concerns. These are the issues that matter. So what matters?

- Purpose matters.
- People matter.
- Participation matters.
- Persistence matters.
- Process matters.
- Possibility matters.

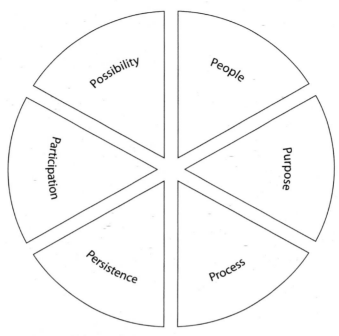

Figure 6.4.   What matters.

Purpose

One explicit theme throughout this book has been the value of linking action to reason. Strategy can be framed, policies written, curriculum developed, and innovations adopted. Absent a compelling reason for following through on the choices and decisions that we make, each will fail. Yet, any reason will not do. Reasons must both resonate with and feel right to the members of the school community. People will become part of and support efforts that inspire them. The success of problem solving rests on engaging people in inspiring, purposeful work. Simply put, purpose turns plans and policies into action. When our purposes are clear our activities are more meaningful.

As our efforts become more meaningful, they become more significant. In turn, people, including faculty and staff, students and parents, are more willing to devote their time and intellect to helping to solve our problems. Shared purpose binds people together in their work. It provides a reason for sticking together through difficult challenges and helps make hard choices easier. When a school's purpose is clearly understood, it serves as a foundation for problem-solving efforts. Purpose matters.

People

At the end of the day, effective problem solving rests on our ability to work well with people. Effective problem solving requires that we are able to communicate our choices and decisions to others. It requires that we are able to involve others in the implementation and evaluation of our actions. It requires that we know how the people in our schools work together to systemically employ programs and policies, innovations, and improvements. The people that matter in and to our schools include faculty and staff, students and parents, and the community that our school serves.

If we fail to pay attention to the people with whom we work we run the risk of losing their trust and respect. If we forget that our primary goal is to educate children and young adults we compromise our ability to achieve the outcomes we value most. If we neglect the assets that parents and the community bring to the problem-solving arena, we make our lives more difficult than they need to be. People matter because they provide us the reason for doing the work we do as well as the resources for completing tasks well.

Participation

We are not in this alone. Furthermore, if we view those who surround us as equal participants in the problem-solving puzzle we are more likely to be successful. By involving others in problem-solving leadership we gain access to their energy, intellect, and expertise. As the old adage states, "Two heads are better than one." In the problem-solving process, intensified effort produces more successful results.

When we encourage participation in problem-solving efforts we expand our pool of resources. Excitement over results is shared, as is progress toward goals. Participation matters because it helps connect the people in the school to problem-solving efforts and deepens their commitment to successful outcomes for students and their learning. As more people are brought into the problem-solving process their participation reinforces communal effort and organizational learning. The outcome is a stronger community, fortified trust in both the school and those that work in it and a foundation for continued effort.

Persistence

Many of the problems school leaders face are not easily solved. The difference is that successful problem solvers stick with their problems, working to understand the nuances of the situation and implementing and evaluating thoughtfully selected solutions. Effective leaders are persistent in their efforts. Rather than trying to find the remedy to their problems, they seek to find remedies that address the complexity of problems their school faces. They choose their focus and then they stick with it. Unless we keep our attention on what matters, we run the risk of finding ourselves off-course. Once off-course, our purposes are diminished and our ability to achieve our goals is weakened.

Persistence does not require that we do the same things again and again; persistence requires that we attend to the same goal in new ways. In this way, we can shift the work we are doing without shifting our goals. Persistence matters because many of the problems school leaders face will endure long past the tenure of even the best school leader. However, progress is possible. As we persist we make small meaningful gains that ultimately create meaningful results.

Process

We can approach each day as if there was nothing to learn from the day before. Or we can work to develop our understandings of how the actions of each member of the school community comprise the whole. Problem solving is a process. Some days it flows. Other days it stalls. Successful leaders understand that if they embrace the ebbs and flows of the process and focus on what they can learn from its highs and lows they can achieve their desired outcomes. Success is, at least in part, a result of sticking with the process.

Not only is problem solving itself a process but it also contains other interwoven processes that contribute to the success or failure of the overall outcome. How we identify problems is a process, how we implement decisions and choices is a process, and how we evaluate our results is a process. Communication, systems thinking, and policy development all are processes that contribute to the success of the problem-solving effort. Effective leaders look at problems as interconnected and, in turn, seek to develop solutions to problems that best interweave the strengths of the school to produce the best possible outcomes and results for students. Process matters. It matters because without attention to the ways in which schools change and learn we cannot capitalize on those efforts in new situations.

Possibility

In the end, whether or not our problem-solving efforts are successful rests as much on our ability to come to work each day ready to meet what faces us as it does on the ways in which we meet our problems. If we see our efforts as futile and our struggle as fruitless, we cannot motivate and lead others. If we view our efforts as productive and our endeavors as contributing, we can inspire and stimulate others to action and accomplishment.

This examination of problem solving started with the claim that *effective problem solving is at the core of great leadership*. For this to be true, effective leaders must see the potential of their problem-solving efforts to positively affect the educational and life outcomes of the students who learn in their schools. They need to believe in working smart as a means to achieve desired outcomes and ends. If we want schools to be better places for students, places where they can learn and grow, we must believe that possibility matters.

IN CONCLUSION . . .

The choices a school leader makes are unavoidably imperfect. However, they change people's lives. Maybe the choices we make don't affect people in big ways all the time. However, it is often the little things that matter the most. Effective problem solving is about taking on the responsibility to make as many good choices as we can. Working smart can help us make better choices.

KEY POINTS

- A school's policy consists of the formal processes and procedures created or adopted by an organization that assure consistent responses to similar situations.
- Policy is influenced by a wide variety of people, with differing understandings of the issues at hand, each with an interest in the outcome that occurs over time and can be influenced by ideas and anxieties far beyond the schoolhouse door.
- Effective leaders develop policy by attending to multiple streams of activity as well as by focusing on and employing the support of community networks.
- Seeking critique and feedback can enhance the policy-development process.
- Attention to purpose, people, participation, persistence, process, and possibility can help leaders work smarter rather than harder.

CHAPTER REFLECTIONS

1. Do the formal policies of your school help or hinder your ability to effectively solve problems? Do informal policies within the school act as barriers or facilitators to the problem-solving process?
2. Are there policies within the school that stand in the way of improvement efforts? What might be done to remove or revise them?
3. What are the greatest areas of need for policy revision or addition?
4. Who are the stakeholders within your school? How is your time spent and invested? How does debate and disagreement impede progress toward valued goals and objectives?
5. How often is critique a part of your school's leadership efforts? When has reflective critique enhanced your school's leadership effort?

CHAPTER ACTIVITIES

All schools have policies. Analyze your school's policies and policy-making processes by completing the following activities.

Activity 1: Analyzing Your Policy Context

Completing a policy context analysis is an important step toward developing effective policy. To do so, first list the formal policies that are present within your school or district (if you're seeking a real challenge try to do both). Group them under the following key themes:

- student behavior, dress code, and nonacademic activities;
- emergencies, school safety, and security;
- technology use across the school and district;
- instructional, curricular, and assessment programs;
- issues of student wellness and nutrition;
- maintenance of property and equipment;
- boundaries of and for attendance, enrollment, transportation, and participation;
- purchasing materials and awarding contracts and agreements for service;
- data collection and analysis;
- curricular reform and innovation;
- problem solving;
- community outreach and involvement;
- governance.

Reflect on the following questions. You may do so by yourself although you might find that engaging others in reflection sheds light on how well your current policies help the school achieve its goals.

1. What does your list reveal about your school?
2. Are the majority of formal policies related to issues of leadership or management?
3. Where are you lacking formal policy?
4. In areas that lack formal policy are there informal agreements about how these issues are addressed?
5. Are the majority of the school policies reactive to problems that have existed in the past?
6. Are there policies that are focused on growth, renewal, and revitalization?
7. Of the policies that are present within the school, which are successful in helping the school achieve its goals? Which are in need of renewal?
8. Are there policies that seem to contradict or complicate other policies? How might they be better aligned?
9. Do redundant policies exist? How might they be streamlined to be better understood and to better support the school?
10. Is there explicit policy that addresses problem-solving activities? In specific, does your school or district have clear policy about data collection and feedback? Implementation efforts? Evaluation efforts? Are there policies about communication? School systems and structures? Policy development? Where might new policies in these areas benefit the school? Who could you count on to help develop such policies?

Activity 2: Discovering Barriers and Facilitators to Effective Policy Development at Your School

To whom can you turn for help creating effective policy? Are the members of your school community muses, critics, or pragmatists? How can you expand your access to resources that can inform your policy-development efforts? How does time affect your ability to create lasting policy? How does debate and disagreement help or hinder the school's progress? Consider what elements are most powerful in your school setting and where they impact the policy-development context by completing the following chart. If you have trusted colleagues, their viewpoints might prove instructive as you probe the policy context of your school.

		Interacting Elements of the Policy Arena			
		Actors	Time	Competing Programs and Policies	Debate and Disagreement
Multiple Streams of Policy Activity	Collection				
	Selection				
	Reflection				

Activity 3: Enhancing Your Problem-Solving Context

Creating a culture of problem solving is an ongoing effort. Start your planning here by outlining your strategies, plans, and approaches.

Problem-Solving Activity	What do you hope to achieve by completing this activity?	Who will be involved?	When will this activity be accomplished?	How will communication on this matter be shared?	How will efforts be evaluated?
Assess your problem-solving orientation					
Assess your school improvement orientation					
Creating space to work smart					
What's your purpose?					
Examine your vision					
READ your school					
Assess your behaviors and activities					
Identify problems in your school					
Initiate actions in your school					

Problem-Solving Activity	What do you hope to achieve by completing this activity?	Who will be involved?	When will this activity be accomplished?	How will communication on this matter be shared?	How will efforts be evaluated?
Evaluate results in your school					
Consider the perspectives of others					
How do you approach negotiation?					
One last communication quiz					
How well is your school linked?					
Consider the ideal					
Lead systems change					
Analyze your policy context					
Discover barriers and facilitators					

Appendix

Aligning ISLLC 2008 with Problem-Solving Content

The ISLLC Standards set the foundation for best practice in educational leadership. Table A.1 illustrates how each of the standards is evidenced in the problem-solving model. Leaders who employ effective problem-solving skills demonstrate their expertise by addressing the learning needs of students and exercising high-quality management skills and behaviors.

Table A.1. Alignment of ISLLC Standards with Chapters

An Education Leader Promotes the Success of Every Student by...	Purpose	The Problem-Solving Model	Talking about Problem Solving	Building Supportive Systems	Problem Solving and School Policy
Standard 1: Facilitating the development, articulation, implementation, and stewardship of a vision of learning that is shared and supported by all stakeholders	A. Collaboratively develop and implement a shared vision and mission	B. Collect and use data to identify goals, assess organizational effectiveness, and promote organizational learning C. Create and implement plans to achieve goals D. Promote continuous and sustainable improvement E. Monitor and evaluate progress and revise plans			
Standard 2: Advocating, nurturing, and sustaining a school culture and instructional program conducive to student learning and staff professional growth	A. Nurture and sustain a culture of collaboration, trust, learning, and high expectations B. Create a comprehensive, rigorous, and coherent curricular program C. Create a personalized and motivating learning environment for students	D. Supervise instruction L. Monitor and evaluate the impact of the instructional program	F. Develop the instructional and leadership capacity of staff	G. Maximize time spent on quality instruction H. Develop assessment and accountability systems to monitor student progress	I. Promote the use of the most effective and appropriate technologies to support teaching and earning

Standard 3: Ensuring management of the organization, operation, and resources for a safe, efficient, and effective learning environment

A. Monitor and evaluate the management and operational systems

B. Obtain, allocate, align, and efficiently utilize human, fiscal, and technological resources

C. Promote and protect the welfare and safety of students and staff

D. Develop the capacity for distributed leadership

E. Ensure teacher and organizational time is focused to support quality instruction and student learning

Standard 4: Collaborating with faculty and community members, responding to diverse community interests and needs, and mobilizing community resources

A. Collect and analyze data and information pertinent to the educational environment

B. Promote understanding, appreciation, and use of the community's diverse cultural, social, and intellectual resources

C. Build and sustain positive relationships with families and caregivers

D. Build and sustain productive relationships with community partners

Standard 5: Acting with integrity, fairness, and in an ethical manner

A. Ensure a system of accountability for every student's academic and social success

B. Model principles of self-awareness, reflective practice, transparency, and ethical behavior

C. Safeguard the values of democracy, equity, and diversity

D. Consider and evaluate the potential moral and legal consequences of decision making

E. Promote social justice and ensure that individual student needs inform all aspects of schooling

Standard 6: Understanding, responding to, and influencing the political, social, economic, legal, and cultural context

A. Advocate for children, families, and caregivers

B. Act to influence local, district, state, and national decisions affecting student learning

C. Assess, analyze, and anticipate emerging trends and initiatives in order to adapt leadership strategies

Sources Cited and Recommended Readings

Adair, J. (2007). *The art of creative thinking: How to be innovative and develop great ideas*. Philadelphia: Kogan Page Limited.

Andersen, B., and T. Fagerhaug (2006). *Root cause analysis: Simplified tools and techniques*. Milwaukee, WI: ASQ.

Ariely, D. (2008). *Predictably irrational: The hidden forces that shape our decisions*. Harper: New York.

Brady, R. (2003). *Can failing schools be fixed?* Washington, DC: Thomas B. Fordham Foundation.

Cohen, H. (2003). *Negotiate this!* New York: Warner Business Books.

Council of Chief State School Officers. (2008). Educational Leadership Policy Standards: ISLLC 2008. http://www.ccsso.org/publications/details.cfm?PublicationID=365 (retrieved May 29, 2008).

Fullan, M. (2001). *Leading a culture of change*. San Francisco: Jossey Bass.

Goodlad, J. (2004). *Romances with schools: A life of education*. New York: McGraw-Hill.

Hale, J. (2001). *Learning while Black: Creating educational excellence for African American children*. Baltimore: Johns Hopkins University Press.

Hord, S. M., and W. A. Sommers (2008). *Leading professional learning communities: Voices from research and practice*. Thousand Oaks, CA: Corwin Press.

Jacob, B. A. (2001). Getting Tough? The Impact of Mandatory High School Graduation Exams on Student Outcomes. *Educational Evaluation and Policy Analysis*. 23(2): 99–121.

Jacob, B., and S. Levitt (2003). Rotten apples: An investigation of the prevalence and predictors of teacher cheating. *Quarterly Journal of Economics*. 118(3): 843–77.

Kotter, J. (1999). *John Kotter on what leaders really do*. Boston: Harvard Business Review.

Kruse, S. D., and K. S. Louis (2009). *Building strong school cultures: A leader's guide to change*. Thousand Oaks, CA: Corwin Press.

Leithwood, K., K. S. Louis, S. Anderson, and K. Wahlstrom, (2004). *How leadership influences student learning*. New York: Wallace Foundation.

Loughran, Regina, and Thomas Comiskey (1999). Cheating the Children: Educator Misconduct on Standardized Tests. *Report of the City of New York Special Commissioner of Investigation for the New York City School District*, December.

Meier, D (1995). *The power of their ideas: Lessons for America from a small school in Harlem*. Boston: Beacon Press.

Mourkogiannis, N. (2006). *Purpose: The staring point of great companies*. New York: Palgrave MacMillan.

Orr, M. T., B. Berg, R. Shore, and E. Meier (2008). Putting the pieces together: Change leadership in an urban low-performing school environment. *Education and Urban Society*. 40(6): 670–93.

Riddel, H. (2007). *Gender, policy and educational change*. New York: Taylor & Francis.

Schmoker, M. (1999). *Results: The key to continuous school improvement*. 2nd ed. Alexandria, VA: ASCD.

Schmoker, M. (2006). *Results now: How we can achieve unprecedented improvement in teaching and learning*. Alexandria, VA: ASCD.

Schultze, C. (1989). Of wolves, termites, and pussycats. *The Brookings Review*. (2) 26–33.

Senge, P. (1990). *The Fifth Discipline*. New York: Doubleday.

Stoll, L., and K. S. Louis (2007). *Professional learning communities: Divergence, depth and dilemmas*. New York: McGraw-Hill.

Tschannen-Moran, M. (2004). *Trust Matters*. San Francisco: Jossey Bass.

Index

About the Author

Sharon D. Kruse is a professor in the Department of Educational Foundations and Leadership at The University of Akron. A national expert on organizational change, Kruse studies school reform and school improvement efforts. She also works with schools and districts as they work to create change. Her recent publications include *Decision Making for Educational Leaders: Under-Examined Dimensions and Issues* (with Bob Johnson Jr.) and *Building Strong School Cultures: A Leader's Guide to Change* (with Karen Seashore Louis).